Naval Mechanical Engineering

Gas Turbine Propulsion, Auxiliary, and
Engineering Support Systems

TANYA D. ZAPATA

authorHOUSE®

AuthorHouse™
1663 Liberty Drive
Bloomington, IN 47403
www.authorhouse.com
Phone: 1 (800) 839-8640

Published by AuthorHouse 08/23/2019

ISBN: 978-1-7283-2417-3 (sc)
ISBN: 978-1-7283-2416-6 (e)

Library of Congress Control Number: 2019912249

Print information available on the last page.

ACKNOWLEDGMENT

This information contained herein has been adapted heavily from *the Gas Turbine System Technician (Mechanical) 3 & 2*, NAVEDTRA 10548 (1988) and *Gas Turbine System Technician (Mechanical) 1 & C*, Volume 2, NAVEDTRA 10549 (1987). Both are in the public domain and were prepared by the Naval Education and Training Program Management Support Activity, Pensacola, Florida, for the Chief of Naval Education and Training. Technical assistance was provided by Naval Sea Systems Command; Service School Command, Great Lakes, Illinois; Naval Surface Warfare School, Newport, Rhode Island; PQS Development Group, San Diego, California; Naval Education and Training Support Center, Pacific, San Diego, California; and Chief of Naval Technical Training, Millington, Tennessee. To the extent, this book does contain text in the public domain; the author does not claim ownership. The author is credited with text compilation and editing. United States Navy photographs were taken by Jason Waite, Jordon R. Beesley, Antonio P. Turretto Ramos, and Paul Farley and released to the public domain.

PREFACE

Naval Mechanical Engineering: Gas Turbine Propulsion, Auxiliary, and Engineering Support Systems are organized to provide information related to the tasks assigned to naval gas turbine technicians. These tasks are required to maintain the ship's engineering plant and to contribute to the comfort of the crew. When we have personnel, who can perform these tasks efficiently, the result is a ship operating at a high state of readiness. The degree of success of the Navy will depend in part on their ability and how they perform their assigned tasks. After all, the primary purpose of training is to produce a combat-ready Navy which can guarantee victory at sea.

CONTENTS

CHAPTER 1

Engineering Support Systems

A naval engineering Gas Turbine Systems Technician (Mechanical) will primarily be assigned to operate and maintain the gas turbine engine. They will also find much of their time concerned with the maintenance and repair of the support or auxiliary systems. The main propulsion plant could not operate without fuel for the engines and lube oil for the reduction gears or saltwater for cooling. All these systems and others are part of the overall main propulsion plant and are your responsibility. They will be assigned to perform Planned Maintenance System (PMS) and repair and to maintain the numerous pumps, valves, and piping associated with these systems. They may also be assigned to the oil lab and be responsible for maintaining and testing the ship's fuels and lubricating oils. On the DD and CG class ships, they will also, as a member of the oil lab, be responsible for the waste heat boiler water chemistry.

In this chapter, you will learn about the various ships' auxiliary systems. You will learn how they are applied to the overall propulsion plant and how the pumps and valves are used in the systems. Since the auxiliary systems vary between ship types, you will learn the systems in general terms. Different classes of ships will be used as examples. The maintenance and upkeep of the auxiliary systems are extremely important since, without them, the main engines would not be able to operate.

FUEL SYSTEM

Gas turbine ships carry two types of fuel aboard — Fuel, Naval distillate NATO symbol F-76 (formerly designated as diesel fuel, marine [DFM]), and JP-5 NATO symbol F-44. Fuel, Naval distillate identifies fuel by MIL-F-16884.

Fuel, Naval distillate is the type of fuel normally used for the gas turbine engines with JP-5 being an alternative fuel that can be used when necessary. While JP-5 may be used for the ship's propulsion plant, its main purpose is for use in the helicopter assigned to the ship for ASW operations. Both fuels must be delivered to the equipment in a clean and water-free state. This is the purpose of the ship's fuel system.

The shipboard fuel system is a method of receiving, storing, purifying, and removing fuel from the ship. The bulk fuel is stored throughout the ship in storage tanks. Fuel is then taken from the storage tanks through the transfer system to the service tanks. The transfer system removes water and contaminants from the fuel and prepares it for use in the gas turbine engine. The service tanks stow the fuel either in use or fuel-ready to be used in the engines. Fuel is taken from the service tanks, through the ship's fuel oil service system where it is further conditioned before use.

Fuel, Naval distillate and JP-5 fuel oil systems are separate systems, both consisting of a fuel oil fill and transfer system and a fuel oil service system. We will discuss these systems separately in the following sections.

NAVAL DISTILLATE SYSTEM

Fuel, Naval distillate is the fuel used for the main propulsion plant on the DD and CG ships. It is also the fuel used for the generators on the DD and CG class ships. Navy distillate is the main type of fuel carried aboard ships.

The Fuel Oil and Transfer System

The Fuel Oil Fill and Transfer System consist of the following components which will be discussed individually.

1. The Fill and Transfer Header
2. Storage Tanks
3. Transfer System

THE FUEL OIL FILL AND TRANSFER HEADER. — The fill and transfer header is a system of piping and valves connecting the main deck filling stations to the storage tanks. This system allows fuel to be taken from the storage tanks to the service tanks. It also provides the capability to defuel the ship.

Fueling and defueling operations begin at the main deck fueling stations. Ships of the gas turbine class have fueling stations forward and aft, which provides the capability of receiving fuel from either the port or starboard side.

Ships are fueled both at sea and in port. The main difference between fueling at sea and in port is the method used to connect the supplying station to the ship. At sea, the probe fueling system is used. The probe method is the most common method used and is standard among ships of the U.S. Navy. Various adapters are available for fueling from ships not equipped with the probe unit. Part of this system is the probe receiver and the hose assembly, which are connected to deck filling connections on the outboard side of the receiving ship. During inport refueling, the supplying activity's hose is bolted to a flanged fitting on board the receiving ship's fueling station.

With the commanding officer's approval, the chief engineer, in conjunction with the oil king, sets up and controls the fueling operation. The oil king aligns the system following EOSS and controls the fueling operation. Standard refueling stations are manned, and the entire operation is monitored from a central point on the ship. Various tests of the fuel are required before, during, and at the securing of fueling. The oil king is responsible for these tests and the reports that must be submitted. These requirements will be discussed in detail in a later chapter.

Fuel flows from the receiving station to the main header pipe and from there to the storage tanks through various valves. On the DD and CG class ships, fuel flows from the deck riser through a motor-operated valve that can be used as a throttling valve to maintain the fuel flow. From there fuel enters the main header and from there to the fuel banks through branch lines. Each fuel bank has its own motor-operated valve. These valves are operated from the fuel console and are either fully opened or fully closed.

The storage tank valves on the DD and CG class ships are electrically operated from the fuel control console located in the central control station (CCS). Except for the manual operation of the valves at the fueling station, the entire fueling operation can be conducted and monitored at the fuel control console. These valves can be opened and closed manually if needed.

STORAGE TANKS. — Fuel storage tanks are nothing more than large enclosed compartments with piping connected to them.

Some ships such as the DD and CG class ships are provided with seawater-compensating systems. With this system, the storage tanks are always kept filled with either fuel or seawater ballast or a combination of both. The receiving tank is connected to a bank of storage tanks using sluice piping between tanks. As a receiving tank becomes full, fuel overflows into the adjoining tank in the bank. This continues until all tanks in the bank are full. During the fueling operation seawater in the tank, bank is displaced by the fuel and is discharged overboard through an overflow line from the overflow expansion tank.

When fuel is taken from the storage tanks for ship's use, on gas turbine ships, seawater from the fire main provides a positive head on the system to the suction side of the transfer pump. Seawater replaces the fuel in the tanks and maintains the proper ship's trim.

CAUTION: Because of the danger of over-pressurizing the ship's receiving system during refueling, the extremely close liaison must be maintained between the receiving ship and the supply ship relative to flow rates and line pressure. Means for throttling flow to each tank bank is provided to prevent tank overpressurization by use of the throttling valve mentioned earlier. A close watch must be kept on liquid levels and receiving tank pressures of banks being filled on ships with compensating systems.

The clean ballast system provides complete separation between ship fuel storage tanks and the seawater ballast system. Tanks designated for fuel storage are used for this purpose only. The fuel fill, transfer, and stripping systems are isolated from drainage, ballast, and bilge systems and are used solely for fuel storage and management. Tanks used for ballast are so designated and can be filled with seawater for ship stability and trim. Designated fuel tanks can be ballasted with seawater through this system whenever the total fuel load is reduced below a set percentage, and additional ballast is required.

The rated full capacity of a fuel tank is 95 percent of the total capacity.

The rated full capacity is computed after allowance has been made for all obstructions in the compartment. The remaining 5 percent of the total tank capacity is reserved to allow for fuel expansion. Accordingly, when fuel is received, tanks should not be filled beyond their rated capacity. This filling requirement does not apply to ships having seawater compensating systems since these tanks are always 100 percent full. Expansion tanks are provided on the DD and CG class ships to provide for fuel expansion caused by temperature changes.

The magnetic-float electric level indicator is used for fuel tanks on newer ships. It is replacing pneumatic-type systems on ships with water-compensating systems because of its improved reliability and accuracy. The Navy oil pollution abatement program requires installation of a magnetic-float level indicator with a high-level alarm in all fuel tanks that overflow directly overboard. This system is installed on newer ships and is slowly replacing the existing static-head gages.

This type of indicator consists of a magnetic float, transmitter (or sensor), and primary and secondary receivers. The transmitter stem is composed of a rod or series of rods mounted vertically within the tank. The magnetic float is cylindrically shaped and has a hole in the center. As it moves up and down on the surface of the fluid, the magnetic float operates tap switches in the rod. The electrical resistance of the transmitter changes according to which rod switches are closed, and this provides an indication of tank level. The float movement is transmitted to a receiver that is calibrated in gallons.

Magnetic-float, liquid-level indicators in tanks that overflow directly overboard have integral, high-level alarms to warn of an impending overboard oil discharge. These alarms are set to sound when the tank has reached 95 percent of total capacity. This alarm point provides the operator with a warning that action must be taken, or the tank will overfill, and that oil will be discharged overboard. On most gas turbine ships; the fuel system is monitored from a central point on the ship. A system control panel consists of gages and alarms that provide information of fuel levels in the tanks; indications of valve alignment; alarms for high and low tank levels; and, in the seawater-compensated system, an alarm for receiving tank overpressurization.

THE TRANSFER SYSTEM

The fuel oil transfer system provides the means of transferring fuel from the storage tanks to the service tanks. In the transfer process, the fuel is cleaned for use in the gas turbine engines. The system consists of transfer pumps, heaters, and centrifugal purifiers.

In the fuel transfer system for the DD class ship, the first step is deciding from which storage bank fuel is to be taken and to which service tank it is to go. Once this is determined, the proper valve can be opened to align the system. Fuel is moved from the storage tank by the transfer pump through the fuel transfer heater. The heater warms the fuel to the proper temperature for cleaning by the purifier. The fuel oil purifier removes water and contaminants as fuel is transferred to the service tanks. Fuel in the service tanks can also be recirculated through the purifier and back to the service tanks by realigning the valves. Fuel must be circulated for a minimum of 3 hours before placing a service tank in operation. This provides a means of continuously reducing the number of solid contaminants in the fuel.

DDs, CG 47, and PHM class ships are being furnished with Self Cleaning Centrifugal Purifiers (SCCPs). The purifier is a vertical, direct drive, centrifugal, self-cleaning (solids ejecting) type of machine that can purify 110 gpm of contaminated diesel fuel, marine. Fuel contaminated with water and solids is fed into the purifier, which separates the pure fuel from the contaminants and returns the purified fuel to the ship's fuel system. The water is continuously passed from the purifier through the ship's piping to a waste oil tank. Separated solids in the form of sludge are retained within the bowl during the cycle. Cleaning the bowl during purifier operation is referred to as "shooting" the bowl. The ejected sludge is also passed to the waste oil system. The purifier can remove water from a contaminated mixture comprised of as much as half water, half fuel. Also, under emergency conditions, the purifier is capable of processing 110 gpm of water for 5 minutes without any water discharge from the oil discharge port.

FUEL OIL SERVICE SYSTEM

Fuel service tanks are like storage tanks except they are not saltwater ballasted. Fuel service tanks have the same type of liquid-level indicating system as other tanks aboard ship. The major concern for the service tanks is cleanliness. The fuel service tanks must be maintained in a clean state of readiness. To maintain cleanliness, you must allow only clean fuel to enter the service tanks.

Fuel Strainers

A wire mesh basket strainer is normally installed between the service tank and the boost pump suction to filter out large solid particles. Fuel enters the top section of the strainer body and is directed into one of the wire-mesh baskets. Large, solid particles are trapped inside the strainer basket and clean fuel travels on through the outlet. Duplex strainers contain two separate strainer housings and baskets and a changeover mechanism that is a shaft with inlet and outlet valves attached to it. As the handle is moved, one set of valves opens, and the other set closes, isolating one strainer assembly. Differential pressure gages and alarm indicators are installed with strainers to alert the operator when the strainer is dirty.

FUEL OIL BOOSTER PUMPS. — Each fuel service system has two booster pumps to provide the system pressure. The fuel booster pump is a vertical screw-type positive displacement pump that is driven by a two-speed electric motor. This type of pump is found on the DD and CG class ships. Directly following the pump discharge is a relief valve. Since the pump is positive displacement, a relief valve is required to protect the system and the pump. The relief valve bypasses fuel back to the pump inlet.

FUEL OIL HEATER. — Fuel oil heaters are installed in the service system after the fuel booster pumps. The heaters are heat exchangers of the conventional shell and U-tube type. Either steam or hot wastewater is used in conjunction with a temperature-regulating valve to maintain the fuel at normal operating temperatures. An alarm is included as part of the system to indicate high fuel temperature to the plant operator.

Filter/Coalescer

The filter/coalescer is the last conditioning station before the fuel is used in the gas turbine engines. The filter/coalescer (hereafter called the coalescer) filters sand, dust, dirt, and scale from the fuel. The coalescer also coalesces water particles and removes all free water essentially from the fuel supplied to the propulsion gas turbines.

The coalescer is a self-contained, static, two-stage unit that combines the process of filtration and water separation in one housing. The basic principle of operation is that contaminated fuel enters the unit through the inlet port and flows into and through the coalescing elements. The flow through the coalescer elements is from the inside to the outside. The coalescer elements remove solid contaminants from the fuel. As the fuel passes through the elements, entrained water coalesces into large droplets that fall to the bottom of the coalescer (sump) where they accumulate.

After passing through the coalescer elements, the fuel passes through the hydrophobic screen and the separator elements, which remove the final traces of coalesced water that have not fallen by their own weight into the sump. The flow through the separator elements is from the outside to the inside. The fuel, free of contaminants, then flows out of the filter/separator through the discharge valve into the fuel system.

When the water/sediment level in the sump reaches a preset level, the automatic drain valve dumps into the water/sediment waste oil system. A sampling valve is provided at the discharge point for testing discharged fuel oil.

As you can see, both the compensated and noncompensated fuel systems are the same in their operation. However, the quality of the fuel must meet stringent requirements to protect gas turbine engines from serious damage, such as corrosion of the hot section, fouling of engine controls, and plugging of fuel nozzles. This level of fuel quality can only be achieved through the continuous purification, sampling, and testing of fuel throughout the system. This is the responsibility of the oil king on board the ship. These requirements will be covered in a separate chapter that discusses the responsibilities of the oil king.

JP-5 SYSTEM

The JP-5 fuel system provides fuel to the helicopter fueling station and the small boat refueling station. It also provides a means of transferring JP-5 to the ship's fuel oil service system under emergency conditions to operate the main engines and generators. On the DD and CG class ships,

JP-5 can be introduced into the system through the system piping just before it enters the fuel oil booster pumps.

The JP-5 system is basically like the ship's fuel oil and transfer system in that it has refueling stations, storage tanks, transfer pumps, service tanks, and filter separators that provide clean fuel to the equipment. Onboard fuel capacity for JP-5 is much less than for Fuel, Naval distillate.

JP-5 is taken on board from topside fueling stations and transferred to the storage tanks. The storage tanks are noncompensated tanks and have the same type of tank level indicators as the Fuel, Naval distillate tanks. Fuel is transferred from the storage tanks to the service tanks through the JP-5 transfer pump and filter separator. The filter separator removes water and contaminants from the fuel before it reaches the service tanks. The transfer piping system also branches off before it reaches the service tanks. This provides JP-5 for emergency use in the ship's fuel system and to the small boat refueling station.

Fuel from the service tanks is used for helicopter refueling and has its JP-5 service pump and filter separator. The service system provides the capability to refuel and recirculate fuel for the helo station. Helo defueling capability is also provided. This capability is necessary because fuel removed from the helo is returned to the storage tanks or diverted to a separate contaminated fuel tank. A stripping pump is provided on both types of ships for removal of water and sludge accumulations on the bottoms of the tanks.

As with the Fuel, Naval distillate, stringent requirements for fuel purity are necessary. The responsibility for testing the fuel again belongs to the oil king.

LUBE OIL FILL, TRANSFER, AND PURIFICATION SYSTEM

The lube oil fill, transfer, and purification system provide the means for storing, transferring, purifying, and heating main reduction gear (MRG) and controllable reversible pitch propeller (CRP) lubricating oil. The major components of this system are the lube oil storage tanks, lube oil settling tanks, lube oil purifier, and the interconnecting piping and valves.

Lubrication reduces friction between moving parts by substituting fluid friction for sliding or rolling friction. Without lubrication, moving a 100-pound weight across a rough surface is difficult; however, with lubrication and proper attention to the design of bearing surfaces, a 1,000,000-pound load can be moved with a motor that is small enough to be held in hand. By reducing friction, lubrication reduces the amount of energy required to perform mechanical actions and reduces the amount of energy that is dissipated as heat.

Lubrication is a matter of vital importance throughout the shipboard engineering plant. Moving surfaces must be steadily supplied with the proper kinds of lubricants. Lubricants must be maintained at specified standards of purity and designed pressures and temperatures in the lubrication systems. Without adequate lubrication, many units of shipboard machinery would quite literally grind to a screeching halt.

The lubrication requirements of shipboard machinery are met in various ways, depending on the nature of the machinery. In the following paragraphs, we discuss the basic principles of lubrication and the lubricants used aboard ship. We also discuss the lubrication systems installed for many shipboard units and the devices used to maintain lubricating oils in the required condition of purity.

FRICTION

The friction that exists between a body at rest and the surface upon which it rests is called STATIC friction. The friction that exists between moving bodies (or between one moving body and a stationary surface) is called KINETIC friction. Static friction, in addition to inertia, must be overcome to put any body in motion. Static friction is greater than the kinetic friction, which must be overcome to keep the body in motion.

The three types of kinetic friction are sliding friction, rolling friction, and fluid friction. Sliding friction exists when the surface of one solid body is moved across the surface of another solid body. Rolling friction exists when a curved body, such as a cylinder or a sphere, rolls upon a flat or curved surface. Fluid friction is the resistance to motion exhibited by a fluid.

Fluid friction exists because of the cohesion between particles of the fluid and the adhesion of fluid particles to the object or medium which is tending to move the fluid. If a paddle is used to stir a fluid, for example, the cohesive forces between the molecules of the fluid tend to hold the molecules together and thus prevent motion of the fluid. At the same time, the adhesive forces of the molecules of the fluid cause the fluid to adhere to the paddle and thus create friction between the paddle and the fluid. Cohesion is the molecular attraction between particles that tends to hold a substance or body together; adhesion is the molecular attraction between particles that tends to cause unlike surfaces to stick together. Regarding lubrication, adhesion is the property of a lubricant that causes it to stick (or adhere) to the parts being lubricated; cohesion is the property that holds the lubricant together and enables it to resist breakdown under pressure.

Different materials possess cohesion and adhesion in widely varying degrees. In general, solid bodies are highly cohesive but only slightly adhesive. Most fluids are highly adhesive but only slightly cohesive; however, the adhesive and cohesive properties of fluids vary considerably.

FLUID LUBRICATION

A liquid is used for most lubrication requirements because, in an enclosed space, a liquid is incompressible. Were it not for this incompressibility, separating moving metal surfaces from each other (preventing metal-to-metal contact) would be impossible. If the lubricant film remains unbroken, sliding friction and rolling friction are replaced by fluid friction.

In any process involving friction, some power is consumed, and some heat is produced. Overcoming sliding friction consumes the greatest amount of power and produces the greatest amount of heat. Overcoming fluid friction consumes the least power and produces the least amount of heat.

Several factors determine the effectiveness of oil film lubrication, including such things as pressure, temperature, viscosity, speed, alignment, condition of the bearing surfaces, running clearances between the bearing surfaces, starting torque, and the nature of purity of the lubricant. Many of these factors are interrelated and interdependent. For example, the viscosity of any given oil is affected by temperature; the temperature is affected by running speed; hence, the viscosity is partially dependent on the running speed.

A lubricant must be able to stick to the bearing surfaces and support the load at operating speeds. More adhesiveness is required to make a lubricant adhere to bearing surfaces at high speeds than at low speeds. At low speeds, greater cohesiveness is required to keep the lubricant from being squeezed out from between the bearing surfaces.

Large clearances between surfaces require high viscosity and cohesiveness in the lubricant to ensure the maintenance of the lubricating oil film. The larger the clearance, the greater must be the lubricant's resistance to being pounded out with consequent destruction of the lubrication oil film.

High unit load on a bearing requires high viscosity of the lubricant. A lubricant subjected to high loading must be sufficiently cohesive to hold together and maintain the oil film.

CLASSIFICATION OF LUBRICATING OILS

The Navy identifies lubricating oils by symbols. Each identification number consists of four digits and, in some cases, appended letters. The first digit indicates the class of oil according to type and use; the last three digits indicate the viscosity of the oil. The viscosity digits are the number of seconds required for 60 milliliters of the oil to flow through a standard orifice at a specified temperature. Symbol 3080, for example, indicates that the oil is in the 3000 series and that a 60-milliliter sample flows through a standard orifice in 80 seconds when the oil is at a specified temperature (210 °F, in this instance). To take another example, symbol 2135 TH indicates that the oil is in the 2000 series and that a 60-milliliter sample flows through a standard orifice in 135 seconds when the oil is at a specified temperature (130°F, in this case). The letters H, T, TH, or TEP, added to a basic symbol number indicate that the oil contains additives for special purposes.

LUBRICATING OIL CHARACTERISTICS

Lubricating oils used by the Navy are tested for a few characteristics, including viscosity, pour point, flash point, fire point, auto-ignition point, neutralization number, demulsibility, and precipitation number. Standard test methods are used for making all tests. The characteristics of lube oil are briefly explained in the following paragraphs.

- Viscosity — The viscosity of an oil is its tendency to resist flow or change of shape. A liquid of high viscosity flows very slowly. For example, in variable climates, automobile owners change oils in accordance with prevailing seasons because heavy oil becomes too sluggish in cold weather and light oil becomes too fluid in hot weather. The higher the temperature of oil, the lower its viscosity becomes; lowering the temperature increases the viscosity.

  The high viscosity or stiffness of the lube oil on a cold morning makes an automobile engine difficult to start. If oil of higher viscosity is used under such conditions, the increased internal friction will raise the temperature and reduce the viscosity of the oil. The viscosity must always be high enough to keep a good oil film between the moving parts—otherwise, there will be increased friction, power loss, and rapid wear on the parts—their viscosities grade oils at certain temperatures. The grade is determined by the number of seconds required for a given quantity (60 milliliters) of the oil at the given temperature to flow through a standard orifice. The right grade of oil, therefore, means oil of the proper viscosity.

- Viscosity index — The viscosity index of oil is based on the slope of the temperature-viscosity curve. The slope of the curve is based on the rate of change in viscosity of a given oil with a change in temperature, but with other conditions remaining unchanged. A low index figure denotes a steep slope of the curve or a great variation of viscosity with a change in temperature; a higher index figure denotes a flatter slope or lesser variation of viscosity with identical changes in temperatures. If you are using an oil with a high viscosity index, its viscosity or body will change less when the temperature of the engine increases.

- Pour point — The pour point of an oil is the lowest temperature at which the oil will barely flow from a container. At a temperature below the pour point, oil congeals or solidifies. A low pour point is an essential characteristic of lube oils used in cold weather operations.

NOTE: The pour point is closely related to the viscosity of the oil. In general, an oil of high viscosity will have a higher pour point than oil of low viscosity.

- Flashpoint — The flash point of an oil is the temperature at which enough vapor is given off to flash when a flame or spark is present. The minimum flash points allowed for Navy lube oils are all above 315 °F, and the temperatures of the oils are always far below that under normal operating conditions.

- Fire point — The fire point of an oil is the temperature at which the oil will continue to burn when ignited.

- Auto-ignition point — The auto-ignition point of an oil is the temperature at which the flammable vapors given off from the oil will burn without the application of a spark or flame. For most lubricating oils, this temperature is in the range of 465 °F to 815 °F.

- Neutralization number — The neutralization number of an oil is the measure of the acid content. It is defined as the number of milligrams of potassium hydroxide (KOH) required to neutralize 1 gram of the oil. All petroleum products deteriorate (oxidize) in the presence of air and heat; the products of this oxidation include organic acids. If organic acids are present in enough concentration, they have harmful effects on alloy bearings at high temperatures, on galvanized surfaces, and the demulsibility of the oil concerning freshwater and seawater. This last effect, in turbine installations, may result in the formation of sludge and emulsions too stable to be broken by the means available. An increase in acidity is an indication that the lubricating oil is deteriorating.

- Demulsibility — The demulsibility, or emulsion characteristic, of an oil, is its ability to separate cleanly from any water present — an important factor in forced-feed systems. Keeping water (fresh or salt) out of oils is especially important.

- Precipitation number — The precipitation number of oil is a measure of the number of solids classified as asphalts or carbon residue contained in the oil. The number is reached by diluting a known amount of oil with naphtha and separating the precipitate by centrifuging — the volume of separated solids equals the precipitation number. The test is a quick means of determining the presence of foreign materials in used oils. An oil with a high precipitation number may cause trouble in an engine by leaving deposits or by plugging up valves and pumps.

SHIPBOARD SYSTEM

The lubricating oil fill, transfer, and the purifying system is used to fill the lubricating oil storage tanks and to transfer lubricating oil between the storage, settling, and sump tanks. It purifies the lubricating oil with the centrifugal oil purifier and preheats the reduction gear lube oil during cold start-up. The system can be set up for either batch purification of one tank or continuous purification using the purifier. The lubricating oil for the reduction gear is the same type as the hydraulic oil for the control reversible pitch system; the purifier is used for both systems.

Storage and Settling Tanks

Replenishment oil for the main reduction gear, controllable reversible pitch propeller system, and in some cases other machinery, is stored in bulk in the lube oil storage tanks. These tanks are filled from a deck connection located near the replenishment stations. These tanks must be kept very clean because the oil stored in them can go directly into either the MRG or the CRP system.

A liquid level indicating system monitors lube oil levels within these tanks. The two components in this system are the transmitter and the indicating meter.

The transmitter is the level detector unit mounted vertically within the tank by brackets or flanges. A magnet-equipped float moves along the transmitter subassembly to vary a voltage, which causes the meter to indicate the number of gallons of oil in the tank.

Storage tanks are nothing more than small enclosed compartments with fill and suction piping connected to them. These storage tanks also have overflow piping attached to prevent overfilling and overpressurizing the tanks.

Settling tanks are like storage tanks except that they have heating coils installed in them to speed up the settling process. Settling tanks allow the oil to stand while accumulated water and other impurities settle to the bottom. The settling action is caused by the difference in specific gravity of the impurities and oil. The force of gravity causes a few layers of contamination to form at the bottom of the tank; the number of layers depends upon the different specific gravities of the contaminants. The heaters not only speed up the settling, but also increase the efficiency of the process.

In Navy ships combined storage and settling tank capacity is two times the combined capacity of the involved lube oil sumps. The recommended lube oil storage on hand is one for one; that is, for each gallon of sump capacity, a gallon should be in on-hand storage.

Purification of Oil

The purity of lubricating oils is essential to the operation of the ship's machinery. Dirt, sludge, water, or other contaminants will act as abrasives to score and scratch metal surfaces within the equipment. Contaminants in oils used for hydraulic applications, such as in the controllable pitch propeller system, could clog small ports and filtering mechanisms in the controls.

Two primary methods of purification are in use at the shipboard level. One method is the batch method, and the other is the continuous method.

BATCH METHOD. — In the batch process, the lubricating oil is transferred from the sump to a settling tank. The oil is heated in the settling tank, and its temperature is maintained at 160°F for 2190 TEP for several hours using steam-heating coils or electric heaters. Water and other impurities are stripped from the settling tank through a drain valve. The oil is then centrifuged and returned to the sump from which it was taken. Alternatively, the oil may be transferred from the sump to a settling tank. The sump tank can be replenished with clean oil immediately by transferring oil from the stowage tank via the purifier. After the oil in the settling tank has been heated, allowed to settle, and then stripped, it is centrifuged and transferred back to the stowage tank.

CONTINUOUS METHOD. — In the continuous purification process, the centrifugal purifier takes suction from a sump tank and, after purifying the oil, discharges it back to the same sump. As the oil passes through a heater, its temperature is raised to the correct level. All oil must be returned to the sump from which it has been taken.

CENTRIFUGAL PURIFIER. — Centrifugal purifiers, frequently called centrifuges, are used extensively in naval service to remove lubricating oil impurities. A centrifuge is a bowl or hollow cylindrical vessel that rotates at high speed while a liquid (in this case contaminated oil) is passed through it. The centrifugal force created by the high rotative speed acts perpendicular to the axis of rotation and causes solid impurities to be deposited on the bowl's inner surface. Water entrained in the oil is segregated in a layer between the solid impurities and the remaining purified oil.

Only materials that are insoluble in one another can be separated in a centrifuge. For example, gasoline and diesel fuel cannot be separated from lubricating oil, nor can salt be removed from seawater, because they are in solution. Water, however, can be separated from oil because water and oil are immiscible (incapable of being mixed). Also, the specific gravities of the materials to be separated must differ. Particle size, fluid viscosity, and the length of the centrifuge period influence the effectiveness of the centrifugal process. In general, the greater the difference in specific gravity between the liquids to be separated and the lower the viscosity of the oil, the greater the rate of separation. Lubricating oils are heated before being centrifuged to decrease their viscosity.

Centrifugal purifiers used on naval ships have bowls of two types, tubular and disc.

1. Tubular type. The tubular type has a small diameter and rotates at a comparatively high speed. The bowl has a three-wing device that keeps the liquid rotating at the speed of the bowl and prevents slippage. The tubular bowl is fed through a nozzle at the bottom.
2. Disc type. The disc type is large in diameter and rotates at a comparatively lower speed. This bowl is fitted with a series of discs that separate the liquid into thin layers. The liquid is ordinarily fed directly toward a series of holes punched through the disc stack; the liquid flows upward through these holes, depending on specific gravity.

In both the tubular and disc types, separated oil moves toward the center for discharge into one of the covers; the separated water moves toward the outside and is delivered from the bowl into the other cover. Solids separated from the liquids are retained in the bowls.

Some ships are being outfitted with a self-cleaning centrifugal purifier whose operation is like the self-cleaning fuel oil purifier. It can purify up to 500 gpm lubricating oil to not more than 0.3 percent water, and not more than 0.02 percent solids.

OIL RENOVATION. — All ships with forced lubrication systems equipped with centrifugal purifiers will operate the purifiers while under way until no visible water remains in the oil and no water is discharged from the purifier. Generally, the main reduction gear lube oil system must be purified 12 hours daily. On gas turbine ships the control reversible pitch oil must be purified for approximately 8 hours with the remaining 4 hours reserved for cleaning the purifier.

When the main propulsion equipment is secured, the lubricating oil should be purified until no water is discharged from the purifier. Also, all oil in the lubrication system should be pumped to the settling tanks and renovated each year.

Sampling Lube Oil

Sampling oil properly is most important in monitoring the lubricating oil because an improper sample produces unreliable test results.

Samples should be representative of the oil to be tested. Sampling containers should be thoroughly cleaned, inspected, and, before use, flushed with the oil to be sampled. All sample containers should be capped promptly after sampling to prevent contamination.

You should observe the following precautions to obtain proper samples.

1. Ensure that uncontaminated, representative samples are obtained.
2. Store unused sampling kits or materials in clean, closed containers.
3. Flush the sampling connection with care. Use, at a minimum, a volume equivalent to the volume of stagnant oil in the connection. If sampling from a sump drain point, be sure to allow enough oil to flow to flush out accumulated water and sediment.

4. If a sample must be taken from equipment after new oil has been added, thoroughly mix the new and old oils by operating the equipment for at least 20 minutes before taking the sample.
5. Use only lint-free wiping cloths to prevent contamination of the lube oil system or the sample.
6. Open the sample bottle only when ready to take the sample; replace the bottle cap immediately after taking the sample.
7. Be sure the sample bottle, cap, or other material is not dropped or pushed into the oil system.

WARNING: If sampling materials are accidentally dropped into the oil sump or tank, do not operate the equipment until they have been removed.

8. Close the valve and replace pipe caps or drain plugs immediately after taking a sample.

Insofar as practical, do not allow the level of lubricating oil in the system to decrease more than 10 percent. Adding small amounts of make-up oil at frequent intervals is a better practice than adding large amounts (over 10 percent) at longer intervals. This practice helps prevent precipitation of decomposition products.

The following procedures should be followed when you are conducting shipboard tests. Ship's force should adhere to the following procedures when conducting shipboard lube oil tests.

1. Draw a lubricating oil sample, as noted above.
2. Check the sample for solid particulate matter by inverting the bottle to see if any sediment or particulate matter falls to the bottom. Hold the bottle inverted for at least 1 minute, then invert again. Repeat this process three times.
3. Visually check the sample to see if the water is present. Lube oil that is free of water has a bright, shiny appearance. Extremely small quantities of free water dull the brightness. As the quantity of entrained water increases, the appearance will change from dull to hazy to cloudy (or milky). Purify oil that is hazy to cloudy.

4. If solid particulate matter is estimated to cover more than one-fourth of the bottom of the sample bottle, purify the oil. Resample and test oil after enough time has been allowed for purification. If oil cannot be purified in a reasonable time, it should be replaced.

5. After testing is completed, deposit lightly contaminated oil into the lube oil settling tank for purification and reuse. Deposit grossly contaminated samples into the contaminated lube oil holding tank. Never dispose of oil samples in the bilges or other pollution-producing areas.

Each ship is required to have a lube oil management program. The lube oil management program consists of two parts.

1. An onboard sampling and testing program.
2. The Navy Oil Analysis Program, which is an off-ship oil test program.

In the onboard lube oil program, all designated operating machinery is sampled periodically. The samples are then compared to samples of the original oil installed in the machinery. A lube oil sample rack is installed in a designated area that contains the sample bottles. The original oil installed in each piece of machinery is sampled. This sample is dated and used as the basis of comparison for all other samples. Samples are taken on the following schedule:

1. Daily — operating machinery at sea or in port
2. Weekly — idle machinery
3. Day before lighting off — all machinery
4. Immediately before getting underway — all machinery
5. Before starting all machinery
6. Day after entering port — all machinery
7. After casualty to machinery
8. When ordered by EOOW/EDO

Generally, the sample rack should contain three sample bottles for each piece of machinery — the original sample, the sample is taken the previous day or week depending on the requirement, and the latest sample taken. A log of all samples taken, and the condition of each sample is maintained and initialed by designated personnel.

The Navy Oil Analysis Program (NOAP) provides spectrometric analysis of ship's lube oil at a designated laboratory. This program can be used to detect accelerated wear in machinery, without the machinery being disassembled, long before any other trouble is indicated. Lube oil samples of selected equipment are submitted to the laboratory periodically for examination. The ship is advised of the test results by the testing activity. The ship maintains accurate records of operating hours after major overhauls, oil changes, and any repairs effected as a result of a recommendation by the laboratory.

We have covered the lube oil fill, transfer, and purifying system in this section. The system that provides lube oil for the reduction gear and CRP system is covered in chapter 10 in the discussion of the power train.

BLEED AIR SYSTEM

Bleed air, as we discussed in the gas turbine engine section, is compressed air taken from ports on different stages of the engines. On all classes of ships, the LM 2500 engine provides customer bleed air for shipboard use from the 16th stage section of the compressor. On the DD, DDG, and CG class ships, bleed air is also provided from the 14th stage of the gas turbine generator compressor. Bleed air is used for several purposes aboard the ship including

1. starting,
2. anti-icing,
3. masker air, and
4. prairie air.

STARTING AIR SYSTEM

Bleed air used for starting is extracted from the compressor section of the gas turbine engine and passes through a regulating valve. The bleed air is regulated at 75 psi and has a temperature of a maximum of 925 °F.

It then enters the bleed air header and is used for the various purposes mentioned above.

The two ship classes use starter air differently; therefore, the systems differ in their method of cooling the bleed air and directing it to the starter.

On the DD, DDG, and CG class ships, bleed air is the primary method of starting the gas turbine engines and generators. The bleed air of the four gas turbine engines and three generators enters a common header and can be used to start any other engine or generator.

Bleed air is taken from an operating engine and generator through the bleed air regulating valve, which reduces the pressure to 75 psi. It then enters the header. The various valves that control the flow can be operated from the PACC in CCS or the PLCC in the engine room. The AUTO MODE can be used to set the valves in sequence during an engine start automatically, or they can be sequenced individually by the operator. The operator can also operate the valve manually by overriding the electrical signal at the valve.

Bleed air for starting goes through two separate pipes. Hot bleed air flows to the mixing valve through the high-temperature bleed air valve. Bleed air also flows through the masker air valve through the masker air cooler where it is cooled to approximately 190°F. The cool bleed air then flows through a filter to remove any solid contaminants and then to the masker/start transfer valve. In the start position, the masker/ start transfer valve allows the cool bleed air to flow to the mixing valve. In the mixing valve, the hot bleed air and cool bleed air are mixed to maintain a temperature of approximately 400 °F to 450 °F. Air then flows through a start air filter and then to the motor air-regulating valve. The motor air-regulating valve regulates start air at approximately 45 psi for starts and 22 psi for motoring. Another valve in the start system is the mixing bypass valve. This valve allows only the cool bleed air to pass to the starter during motoring.

Start air on the DD, DDG, and CG class ships flows from the engine into a common header through a reducing valve where it is reduced to 75 psi. It then passes through the bleed air cooler, which maintains the air at a temperature of approximately 400 °F; from there it passes to the start air system and to the motor air-regulating valve.

ANTI-ICING AIR

The anti-icing systems on the different classes of ships differ greatly and will be covered separately.

DD, DDG, CG Class Anti-Icing

The gas turbine anti-icing systems take hot bleed air from the bleed air header and distribute it to each GTM and GTGS intake to prevent the formation of ice under an icing condition. An icing condition exists when the inlet air temperature to a gas turbine engine is 41 °F or less and the humidity of the inlet air is 70 percent or greater.

Bleed air from the header enters the anti-icing system piping for each GTM and GTGS and is directed to the anti-icing, air flow regulating valves. The forward and after bleed air header risers provide the hot bleed air for each GTM and GTGS in number 1 and number 2 engine rooms. The bleed air header in number 3 generator room provides the hot bleed air for the number 3 GTGS. The anti-icing, air flow regulating valves control the flow of hot bleed air into the intake of each gas turbine engine. This maintains the temperature of the inlet air to each gas turbine engine at + 38 °F, or greater, during engine operation. Each valve is a double-pneumatic, piston-actuated, butterfly-vane, regulating-type valve. This valve is electronically controlled by an associated anti-icing temperature controller. These controllers are enabled or disabled by the seven anti-icing ON/OFF push-button switch indicators on the PLCC's and PACC.

The controller used to operate the anti-icing valve for each GTM intake combines and compares three signals with the fixed temperature signals. (The three input signals are ambient-air temperature, gas generator speed and bulk-air temperature. The fixed temperature signals are +38 °F or bulk-air temperature. The comparison of these signals determines the torque motor control positioning signal. This signal drives the anti-icing valve torque motor, which positions a poppet valve in the valve's pneumatic regulating control assembly. The poppet valve, in turn, regulates the amount of pressure the 100 psig ship's service air can exert on the valve's pneumatic actuating pistons; the position of the pistons determines the valve setting. When ship's service air pressure on the pistons is not working, a spring in the valve's actuator assembly maintains the valve's butterfly vane in the closed position.

When the GTM anti-icing temperature controller is enabled, it maintains the temperature of the inlet air in the intake at + 38 °F. The controller maintains this temperature by comparing bulk air temperature to the controller's +38°F fixed temperature reference. However, when changes in engine speed are made, the speed sensor (N_{GG}) signals the controller to immediately complement the increase or decrease in intake air flow with a corresponding increase or decrease in hot bleed air flow. The ambient air temperature sensor signal determines the magnitude of valve position change that will accompany any given engine speed change. Following an engine speed change, the controller will again regulate the temperature of the inlet air in the intake to +38°F by comparing the bulk air temperature to the controller's + 38°F fixed temperature reference.

The controller used to operate the anti-icing valve for each GTGS intake combines and compares one input signal (duct air temperature) with the fixed temperature signals (+ 38°F) to produce a torque motor control position signal. The anti-icing valve used on a GTGS is the same as that used on a GTM.

When the GTGS anti-icing temperature controller is enabled, it maintains the temperature of the inlet air in the intake at + 38 °F. Again, the controller compares duct air temperature to the + 38°F fixed temperature.

After the bleed air passes the anti-icing, air flow regulating valves, it becomes anti-icing air and is piped to the engine intakes. Anti-icing air entry into a GTGS intake is made through an eight-inch pipe. The hot anti-icing air flows into the intake duct and mixes with the intake air. No manifolds or nozzles are used.

Injection of hot anti-icing air into the GTM intakes is accomplished through the U-shaped manifolds mounted at the 02 level above the silencers inside each duct. The manifolds are constructed from eight-inch diameter pipe with 1 1/4-inch holes drilled along the sides of each leg. Because of the larger cross-sectional area and capacity of the propulsion intakes, the manifold must be used to mix the air thoroughly.

MASKER AIR

Because of the existing differences between classes, the system will be covered separately.

DD, DDG, CG Masker Air

The masker air system takes hot bleed air from the bleed air system, cools it to 190°F, and distributes it to the masker emitter rings outside the ship's hull. This reduces or modifies the machinery noise being transmitted through the hull to the water.

Bleed air at approximately 500 to 800 °F and at 75 psig from the bleed air header enters the masker air system within each engine room and is directed to the masker air cooler valve. After the hot bleed air has passed through the masker cooler valve, it is piped to the masker air cooler where it is cooled to 190°F. The masker air cooler is a shell and tube-type cooler which uses seawater as the cooling medium. The cooled masker air is piped through to the masker air filter to remove any solid contamination and then to the masker/start transfer valve. The masker/start transfer valve controls the flow of the 190°F masker air to either the masker air system or to the gas turbine start/motor air system. Push buttons at the control consoles or, in an emergency, manual override can be used to select the position of the valve.

After the masker air passes through the masker/start transfer valve, it is piped to the masker air pressure-regulating valves. The regulating valve maintains a 30 psig regulated pressure in the masker emitter ring flow manifolds. Masker air then passes into the emitter flow distribution manifold. As the masker air leaves the manifold and enters each branch line, it passes through a flowmeter orifice to a manual flow control valve. The flowmeter orifice creates the differential pressure required to operate its associated flowmeter. The manual flow control valve establishes the prescribed masker air flow to its respective emitter ring. From the manual flow control valve, masker air continues through a check valve and a shutoff valve. It then flows into the hollow emitter ring on the ship's outer hull. The emitter ring has a series of 1/16-inch diameter holes in its outer wall through which the air escapes.

PRAIRIE AIR

The prairie air system modifies the thrashing noise produced by the ship's propellers to disguise the sonar signature of the propellers. The system does this by taking hot bleed air from the bleed air header, cooling it, and distributing it to the leading edges of the propeller blades.

The prairie air system is basically the same on all classes of gas turbine ships. Bleed air is directed from the header to a prairie air cooler by the prairie air valve. On the DD, DDG, and CG class ships, the prairie air valve is operated from the control console. The bleed air is cooled to 100 °F on the DD, and so forth. These are the maximum prairie air temperatures. An alarm indication is given when these temperatures are exceeded.

A manually operated flow valve is used to establish the prescribed prairie air flow to the propeller. From the prairie air, flow control valve, prairie air is piped to the oil distribution box on the front of the main reduction gear. At the oil distribution box, the prairie air enters the propeller shaft through a roto seal and travels through the shaft to the propeller blade. It then enters the water through a series of holes on the leading edge of each blade.

SEAWATER SERVICE SYSTEMS

The seawater service system is the ship's principal cooling water system. This system distributes seawater throughout the engineering plant at prescribed pressures and flow rates for cooling lubricating oils, compressed air, and auxiliary machinery. Although the different classes of ships provide the same basic services, they are set up differently. Therefore, they will be discussed individually.

DD, DDG, CG Seawater Systems

During normal operations, seawater is sup plied to the seawater service system main through the three firemain reducing stations. When seawater service system demand increases, the seawater pumps are used to supply the seawater service system main.

The systems on all the ships are basically the same but do differ in several ways. The basic system consists of three seawater service pumps that supply cooling water to a variety of equipment. These pumps are centrifugal-type pumps that can be controlled locally at their respective motor controllers or remotely from the PACC. These pumps take suction through a sea chest and then through a hydraulically operated valve. This valve is controlled from the damage control deck. It is used in case of damage to the system piping to prevent flooding from the sea. This valve can also be manually overridden at the valve location. From there flow is through a manual suction valve, a manual discharge valve, and a check valve that is used to prevent backflow to the pump. Relief valves protect the seawater system and associated equipment from over-pressurization.

Reducing stations are provided on the DD class ships to reduce pressure for use on the various equipment. However, because of design modifications to the system pressure on the CG class ships, reducing stations have been eliminated. The only exception is firemain-to-seawater-system reducing stations and a reducing station for the CRP cooler.

Various pressure settings on the relief valves and reducing stations and system pressure itself vary between ships. The EOSS should be consulted for proper settings and alarm conditions.

Temperature regulation of the reduction gear lube oil cooler, control of the waste heat boiler condensers, and the condensate drain coolers is done by pneumatically operated temperature regulators. These regulators control the flow of seawater through the coolers to maintain the temperature of the liquid being cooled within prescribed limits. In addition, the CG class ships have a CRP cooler that is also temperature regulated.

Nine manual/hydraulic operated butterfly valves are associated with the seawater service system. Three of these valves control the flow of seawater to the three seawater pumps, as mentioned previously. Six valves are installed at various locations along the seawater service main to control the flow of seawater through the main.

Different types of strainers are in the system to prevent marine growth and system contamination.

The seawater main also provides backup cooling to the ship service generators. In case the generator cooling system fails, the seawater main automatically cuts in.

AUXILIARY COOLING SYSTEM. — The firemain also provides direct seawater cooling to various nonpropulsion auxiliary equipment. Such equipment includes the low-pressure (LP) and high-pressure (HP) air compressors, air-conditioning plants, refrigeration plants, and some electronic cooling water systems. The fire main in the engine room provides cooling water to the propulsion, gas turbine, bleed air cooler, the prairie air cooler, and the gas turbine starting/motoring air cooler. The firemain in AMR number 3 provides filtered seawater for cooling, lubricating, and flushing the stern tube shaft seal and the stern tube bearing.

COMPRESSED AIR SYSTEMS

Compressed air systems consist of the high-pressure air system and the ship's service air system or low-pressure air system. The systems vary between ships and classes and are described in the following sections.

DD, DDG, CG Low-Pressure Air System

The ship's service air system is the general-purpose air system. It provides low-pressure air throughout the ship for operation of nearly all pneumatically operated equipment and pneumatic controls. It supplies purified low-pressure air to the electronics and to the high-pressure air system dryers. The following are examples of the uses of LP air in the engineering plant:

1. Fuel oil fill and transfer compensating system
2. Waste heat boiler control air
3. Seawater temperature control valves
4. Fuel oil coalescer
5. Clutches and/or brakes

The system consists of LP air compressors, air dryers, purifiers, main receivers, and a piping system. The piping system consists of valves, reducing stations, and connections necessary to distribute compressed air to various services. A reducing station is provided in the high-pressure air system to supplement the ship's service air when compressed air consumption exceeds ship's compressor output. Automatic shutoff valves, called priority valves, are installed downstream from all mission essential equipment and upstream from all nonessential services. In the event air pressure falls below a prescribed setting, these valves close and eliminate use of non-essential services during the reduced pressure period.

Ships have so many variations as to the type and number of compressors, the system pressure settings, and priority valve settings that we will not attempt to cover this material. Refer to ship's equipment technical manuals and EOSS for a more in-depth description of each individual system.

DD, DDG, CG High-Pressure Air Systems

The high-pressure air system provides HP air to the weapons systems, aviation equipment, and gas turbine starting and backup for the ship's service air system.

The system consists of two compressors that supply 3,000 psig of air to the storage flask. The air then goes into the system through a dehydrator. The dehydrator provides moisture-free, oil-free, and contaminant-free air to the system.

The HP air system is primarily maintained by A-Division. The naval engineering Gas Turbine System specialist will find its use in the engine room as the emergency air start for the ship's main engines and generators. HP air flasks are in each engine room and number 3 generator room. Air for the main engine start is reduced to 250 psig by the HP reducing valve and then to 85 psig through a series of orifices. The DDG does not have HP air start capability for its main engines. The CG class pressures are 220 psig through the reducing valves and 45 psig through the orifices. All ships have HP air start capability for the ships' generators. The 3,000 psig of air is reduced to starting pressure by the start air valve. The 3,000 psig of air is also used to back up the LP air supply through a reducing station in the number 1 engine room. The pressure varies between ships. EOSS should be consulted for proper settings.

SUMMARY

We have covered the functions and operations of several auxiliary or support systems for the gas turbine ships. specialist will need to become familiar with all these systems to properly operate the engineering plant. While the main engines are the heart of the engineering plant, without the support systems the ship would not operate.

As you can see in reading through this chapter, the various temperatures and pressures vary greatly between systems; the systems themselves vary between classes and even between ships of the same class. They mostly study their own ship's engineering plant and read the ship's EOSS and technical manuals to be able to operate, repair, and maintain their individual ship's equipment.

REFERENCES

- S9FFG-AL-POG-010, Propulsion Operating Guide
- S9234-AL-GTP-010/DD-963 PPM Plant Pro pulsion Manual
- S9234-AL-GTP-030/DD-963 PPM Plant Pro pulsion Manual
- NAVSHIPS 0905-496-3010, Propulsion Operating Guide
- S9CGO-BP-POG-010/CG47CL, Propulsion Operating Guide
- NAVEDTRA 10097, Marine Gas Turbine Operations
- Naval Ships' Technical Manual 262 Naval Ships' Technical Manual 541 Naval Ships' Technical Manual 542

CHAPTER 2

Propulsion Systems
And Power Train

As naval engineers advance in their careers, more is expected of them as a leader and a technician. They find that more of their time is spent in training and motivating their subordinates than working on equipment.

This chapter presents some of the various factors that affect gas turbine performance, procedures for engine changeout, and power train inspection.

Numerous reference materials will be cited to indicate the referenced manuals naval engineers read to amplify the subjects covered, increase their technical knowledge, and provide them with the information to properly do their job and train their subordinates.

ENGINE PERFORMANCE AND EFFICIENCY

Gas Turbine System Technician (Mechanical) prime concern is to keep the machinery for which you are responsible operating in the most efficient manner possible. From their previous experience and training, they know that there are many variables which affect engine performance. As they continue to gain experience and understanding, they will be expected to train their subordinates and pass this knowledge to them. Some of the questions they will be asked during these training sessions will be why an engine does or does not perform efficiently. They must be able to answer these and many other questions through their knowledge and use of reference texts.

To understand the various factors that in fluence engine performance, a thorough understanding of basic physics concepts is necessary. Once the physics concepts are understood, it will be much easier for you to appreciate the part played by such factors as compressor and turbine design, engine operating conditions, fuel characteristics, ignition, pressures, temperatures, and compression ratios.

PHYSICS CONCEPTS

In this section we will briefly discuss the various elements of power, speed, and mass; how they relate to each other; and how they relate to engine operation.

Force

Force is defined as a push or pull which will produce or prevent motion. Gravity, for example, is a force that attracts bodies toward the earth at a rate that will cause the object to increase its velocity by 32.2 feet per second (fps) for each second the object is falling; that is, at the end of 2 seconds the speed would be 64.4 fps, at the end of 3 seconds, 96.6 fps, etc. The figure 32.2 fps^2 is called the acceleration due to gravity and is represented in formulas by the letter g. This value can also be used to determine the amount of resistance an object of given weight offers to motion. By dividing the weight by the acceleration constant, the resulting quotient is the mass of the object.

EXAMPLE: $M = \dfrac{W}{g}$

Force is also a vector quantity; that is, it has both magnitude and direction. When we speak of 1,000 pounds of force acting upon an object, we cannot know its effect unless we know the direction of the force. Two or more forces acting on a body will produce a resultant force.

Work

Work is produced when a force acting on a body causes it to move through a distance.

Thus:

Work = force x distance

or

W = Fd

It is important to remember that work is accomplished only when an object is moved some distance by some force. For example, if an object that is pushed as hard as possible fails to move, then by textbook definition, no work has been done.

Force is most often expressed in pounds, distance in feet, and work in foot-pounds.

EXAMPLE:

An engine that is exerting 1,000 pounds of force moves its vehicle 10 feet. How much work is being accomplished?

Work = Fd
      = 1,000 x 10
      = 10,000 ft-lb

Power

Nothing in the definition of work states how fast the work is being done. The rate of doing work is known as power.

$$Power = \frac{force \times distance}{time}$$

or

$$P = \frac{Fd}{t}$$

Power may be expressed in any one of several ways, depending upon the units used for the force, the distance, and the time. Power is most often expressed in units of horsepower. One horsepower is equal to 33,000 foot-pounds per minute or 550 foot-pounds per second. In other words, a 1-hp motor can raise 33,000 pounds 1 foot in 1 minute or 550 pounds in 1 second.

$$hp = \frac{power\ (ft\text{-}lb/min)}{33,000} \qquad hp = \frac{power\ (ft\text{-}lb/sec)}{550}$$

or

$$= \frac{Fd/t\ (min)}{33,000} \qquad = \frac{Fd/t\ (sec)}{550}$$

EXAMPLE:

A 5,000-pound weight is lifted a distance of 10 feet in 2 minutes. How much horsepower is required?

$$P = \frac{Fd}{t}$$

$$= \frac{5,000 \times 10}{2}$$

$$= 25,000\ ft\text{-}lb/min$$

$$hp = \frac{P}{33,000}$$

$$= \frac{25,000}{33,000}$$

$$= 0.75\ or\ 3/4$$

Energy

Energy is the capacity for doing work. The energy which bodies possess is classified into two categories—potential and kinetic. Potential energy is stored energy which may be due to (1) its position, such as water in an elevated storage tank; (2) distortion, such as a compressed spring; or (3) chemical composition (coal, for example).

Potential energy is computed by the following formula: where the weight of an object or the force exerted against an object is known, and the distance is known

PE = potential energy, ft-lb

W or F = weight or force, lb

H = height of object; feet, inch, and so forth.

For example, a coil spring is compressed 2 inches by a weight of 600 pounds. How much potential energy does this spring possess?

PE = WH
   = 600 x2
   = 1,200 in-lb or 100 ft-lb

Kinetic energy is energy in motion. Gases striking a turbine wheel is an example of kinetic energy. If the mass and speed of a body is known, the kinetic energy can be determined from the following formula:

$$KE = \frac{WV^2}{2g}$$

Where
W = weight, lb
V = 0velocity, fps
g = acceleration due to gravity = 32.2 fps^2
KE = kinetic energy, ft-lb

Notice that kinetic energy is directly proportional to the square of the velocity.

EXAMPLE:

A vehicle weighing 3,500 pounds has a velocity of 60 mph (88 fps). What is the kinetic energy?

$$KE = \frac{WV^2}{2g}$$

$$= \frac{3,500 \times 88^2}{2 \times 32.2}$$

= 420,869.56 ft-lb of energy

Speed

Speed, by definition, is distance traveled per unit of time. In the Navy these units are most commonly expressed in knots, miles per hour, and feet per second.

Speed = $\dfrac{\text{distance}}{\text{time}}$

Velocity

Velocity can be defined as speed in a given direction and is expressed by the letter V in equations.

Acceleration

The acceleration of a body in motion is defined as the rate of change of its velocity. This definition is not based on the distance traveled, but on the loss (deceleration) or gain (acceleration) of velocity with time.

Acceleration = $\dfrac{\text{change in motion}}{\text{unit of time}}$

$\qquad = \dfrac{\text{final velocity minus initial velocity}}{\text{time}}$

$\qquad = \dfrac{V_2 - V_1}{t}$

where V_1 is initial velocity and V_2 is final velocity

Mass

The mass of an object is the amount of fundamental matter of which it is composed; it is, in a sense, the measure of a body's inertia.

Mass and weight are often confused because the common method of determining a quantity of matter is by weight. But weight is only the measure of the pull of gravity on a quantity of matter. An object that weighs 36 pounds on the earth will only weigh 6 pounds on the moon, yet the mass is the same. Mass is derived by dividing the weight of the object by the acceleration due to gravity (as previously stated, is equal to 32.2 fps² on earth).

$$M = \frac{W}{g}$$

Momentum

Mass times velocity, or MV, defines momentum. It is the property of a moving body that determines the length of time required to bring it to rest under the action of a constant force. Large objects with a lot of mass but very little velocity can have as much momentum as low-mass objects with a very high velocity. A ship must dock very slowly and carefully because if it touches the dock even gently, it may crush it. On the other hand, a bullet weighs very little, but its penetrating power is very high because of its velocity.

FACTORS EFFECTING ENGINE PERFORMANCE

Gas turbine engines are more sensitive to operating variables than are most other types of engines. Such variables can generally be divided into two groups — those that change because of design or operating characteristics of the engine and those that change because of the medium in which the engine must operate.

Design factors include the following:

- Engine speed
- Size of nozzle area
- Weight of fuel flow
- Amount of bleed airflow from the compressor
- Turbine inlet temperature

Nondesign factors include the following:

- Temperature of the air

- Pressure of the air
- Density of the air
- Relative humidity
- Cleanliness of the compressor

Only engine speed and the nondesign factors will be discussed. The effect of the other variables on engine operation is not discussed.

Speed

Engine speed in revolutions per minute (rpm) has a great effect on the power developed by the engine. Very little power is developed at low engine rpm as compared to the power developed at high engine rpm, and that a given rpm change has more effect on engine power at higher engine speeds than at lower engine speeds. The amount of air pumped by a compressor is a function of compression speed. An increase in the amount of air being pumped will result in an increase in power.

Temperature

Gas turbine engines are very sensitive to variations in the temperature of the air. All engines used by the Navy are rated on a standard day, which is an air temperature of 100°F, 29.92 in.Hg barometric pressure, and 0 percent relative humidity. If the engine operates in temperatures hotter than standard, less power will be produced. Conversely, engine operation in air temperatures colder than standard day conditions will result in more power being produced.

A rise in ambient temperature will cause the speed of the air molecules to increase so that they run into each other harder and move further apart. When the molecules are further apart, a given number of them will occupy more space. Therefore, not as many can get into the engine inlet area. This results in a decrease in the amount of the air into the engine with a corresponding decrease in power.

Temperature Changes Through the Engine

Air entering the compressor on a standard day is at a temperature of 100°F. Due to compression, the temperature through the com pressor gradually climbs to a point that is determined by the number of compression stages and its aerodynamic efficiency. On some large engines, the temperature at the front of the combustion section is about 600 °F. As the air enters the combustion chambers, fuel is added, and the temperature is raised to about 3,500 °F in the hottest part of the flame. Since this temperature is above the melting point of most metals, the combustion chamber and surrounding parts of the engine are protected by a film of air which is established by the design of the combustion chamber. Because of this air film, the air entering the turbine section is considerably cooler. The acceleration of air through the turbine section further reduces the temperature as the thermal energy is converted into mechanical energy.

Pressure

An increase in pressure results when there are more molecules per cubic foot. When atmospheric pressure increases, there are more molecules available to enter the engine inlet area; and as a result, an increase in the amount of air occurs through the engine. Since marine gas turbines operate at sea level, atmospheric pressure changes have a minimal effect on engine operation.

PRESSURE CHANGES. — Air usually enters the front of the compressor at a pressure that is slightly less than ambient, due to the very high suction at the inlet to the engine. From this point on, there is a considerable pressure rise through the successive compression stages, with the rate of rise increasing in the later stages of compression. The exit area of the exhaust, the exit area of the turbine nozzles, and the number of compression stages all have an influence on the compression ratio of the compressor. A final pressure rise is accomplished in the divergent section of the diffuser. From the diffuser, the air passes to the combustion section where a slight pressure loss is experienced. The combustion-chamber pressure must be lower than the com pressor discharge pressure during all phases of engine operation to establish a direction of airflow toward the rear of the engine and allow the gases to expand as combustion occurs. A sharp drop in pressure occurs as the air is accelerated through the converging passages of the turbine nozzle. As the gases pass through the diverging turbine blades, pressure increases slightly and then drops again through the next set of nozzles. This process continues through all the turbine stages. The pressure continues to drop to near ambient at the exhaust.

COMPRESSION RATIO. — In all types of compressors, the compression ratio (C/R) is equal to the compressor discharge pressure (CDP) divided by the compressor inlet pressure (CIP). Or mathematically

$$CR = \frac{CDP}{CIP}$$

This ratio represents a pure number and is normally expressed by the number obtained through the above division to one; i.e., 16 to 1, or 16:1. This would signify a compressor that raises the pressure of the incoming air 16 times. In this case, if the incoming air were at a pressure of 10 psia, the CDP air would be at a pressure of 160 psia.

Since we are primarily interested in the axial flow types of compressors, we will now take a more in-depth look at their compression ratios.

It has been determined that the maximum compression ratio per any stage in an axial flow compressor is approximately 1.2 to 1. When higher ratios are attempted, increased forces and turbulence result, which causes low efficiency.

If we know the compression ratio per stage and the number of stages a compressor has, we can then determine the overall compression ratio of the compressor. Although the pressure ratio remains unchanged across each stage, the pressure rise varies across each stage. The following is an example. A 13-stage compressor has a pressure ratio at each stage of 1.1:1 and an ambient inlet of 14.7 psi.

To determine the final pressure and the overall pressure ratio we use the following computations:

STAGE 1 STAGE 2 STAGE 3
14.7x1.1 = 16.17x1.1 = 17.79 x 1.1

STAGE 4 STAGE 5 STAGE 6
= 19.57 x 1.1 = 21.51 x 1.1 = 23.67 x fl

STAGE 7 STAGE 8 STAGE 9
= 26.04 x 1.1 = 28.65 x 1.1 = 31.51 x 1.1

STAGE 10 STAGE 11 STAGE 12
= 34.66 x 1.1 = 38.13 x 1.1 = 41.94 x 1.1

STAGE 13
= 46.13 x 1.1 = 50.75

FINAL PRESSURE = 50.75 psi

INITIAL PRESSURE = 14.7 psi

Compression ratio = $\dfrac{50.73}{14.7}$ = 3-45:1

The pressure rise across the first stage is

16.2 psi pressure at back of 1st stage
- 14.7 psi pressure at front of 1st stage
1.5 psi pressure rise across 1st stage

Pressure rise across the last stage is

50.75 pressure at back of 13th stage
- 46.13 pressure at front of 13th stage
4.62 pressure rise across 13th stage

The pressure ratio is the same for each stage, but the pressure rise is greater at the last stage. The velocity and density influence pressure rise through a compressor. Compression ratio will increase or decrease with engine speed. The compressor inlet temperature will also influence pressure rise through the compressor.

VARIABLE GEOMETRY COMPRESSORS. — In some axial flow compressors, a variable geometry compressor may be used. In this case, the inlet guide vanes are used to change angle (schedule) during engine operation at different speeds and under different temperature and pressure conditions.

When these vanes can schedule, the effective angle of attack of the blades on the air is changed (due to the direction of the air into the blades having been changed by the variable vanes). When this occurs, the compression ratio per stage will be different. Since the basic purpose of the variable vanes is to lower the angle of attack in the first stages, the compression ratio per stage will be less in the first stages.

In axial flow compressors, the total amount of air flowing through the compressor is not changed by the addition of stages, but the overall compression ratio is. To increase the overall compression ratio of an axial flow compressor, we add more compressor stages.

Density

Density is defined as the number of molecules per cubic foot. It is affected by both temperature and pressure. When the pressure goes up, the density goes up; and when the temperature goes up, the density goes down. This is expressed mathematically as fuel control does not measure the volume of air directly, but measures fuel flow as a function of pressure, temperature, and rpm.

Compressor Cleanliness

The cleanliness of the compressor blading has a very large effect on overall engine performance and efficiency. If salt deposits, oil mist, and dirt can accumulate on the blades, the result will be an increase in engine vibration and a decrease in airflow and compression. With the decreased airflow, turbine inlet temperatures will increase, and power will decrease. If this condition is allowed to continue, the ultimate result will be poor fuel efficiency, shorter engine life, and a greatly increased possibility of compressor stall. Frequent cleaning of intake air trunks and water washing the GTE will reduce the possibility of compressor stall and increase engine efficiency.

$$\text{Density ratio} = K = \frac{P}{T}$$

Where

K = a constant

P = pressure, in.Hg

T = temperature, °R

Density is directly proportional to pressure and inversely proportional to temperature times a constant. A constant of 18.71 is necessary in order to make the density ratio equal 1 under standard day conditions of temperature (560 °R) and pressure (29.92 in.Hg).

$$\text{Density ratio} = K\frac{P}{1}$$

$$= 18.71\frac{29.92}{560}$$

$$= 1$$

°R is determined by adding 460 to °F.

Humidity

Humidity has a negligible effect on the GTE. Since water vapor weighs only five-eighths as much as dry air, an increase in humidity will decrease the weight per unit volume. The GTE fuel control does not measure the volume of air directly, but measures fuel flow as a function of pressure, temperature, and rpm.

Compressor Cleanliness

The cleanliness of the compressor blading as a very large effect on overall engine performance and efficiency. If salt deposits, oil mist, and dirt can accumulate on the blades, the result will be an increase in engine vibration and a decrease in airflow and compression. With the decrease in airflow, turbine inlet temperatures will increase, and power will decrease. If this condition can continue, the ultimate result will be poor fuel efficiency, shorter engine life, and a greatly increased possibility of compressor stall. Frequent cleaning of intake air trunks and water washing the GTE will reduce the possibility of compressor stall and increase engine efficiency.

COMPONENT CHANGEOUT

Gas turbine powered ships are outfitted with all the equipment necessary to remove and replace engine components. As a senior petty officer, you will be supervising component changeouts. As with any job you must plan and organize before starting the project. Since most GTE problems occur while the ship is underway, corrective maintenance has to be performed immediately. If you insist upon strictly following step-by-step procedures as set forth in the technical manual, you will save' time by preventing errors. Do not rely upon memory for component changeout; memories are fallible.

PREPARATIONS

Before changing components on a GTE, ensure that the replacement parts and tools to accomplish the job are available and that you have read the proper technical manual procedures.

A method you can use to ensure that personnel follow the technical manual procedures is to provide them with a copy of the procedure and instruct them to check off each step as it has been accomplished. Inspect all measuring devices (such as torque wrenches, meters, and micrometers) to ensure they are in calibration.

ESTIMATED TIME OF REPAIR

When making an estimated time of repair (ETR), you must be as accurate as possible because your ETR could ultimately affect the operational schedule of the ship. Take into account all the factors that may affect an ETR, such as capabilities of your personnel, availability of materials, test procedures, preparations, and time for unexpected delays.

REPLACEMENT

As a supervisor your primary concern is for the safety of your personnel and equipment. As a responsible petty officer, you set the example. Do not allow short cuts around safety precautions to save time. You can prevent accidents and save time by explicitly following safety precautions and actively using safety programs such as tag-out and electrical safety.

During component changeout, keep track of tools going into and out of the GTE enclosure. Ensure that your personnel use care when removing lockwire, cannon plugs, and so forth. Tag and bag all bolts, nuts, washers, and interferences that are removed for reinstallation. Capping fluid lines will prevent contamination of open systems. Use care when replacing GTE components. Most problems that arise after component replacement are usually caused by careless work and not properly following the procedure from technical manuals.

COMPLETION OF REPAIRS

After GTE repairs are complete, you must ensure that the proper entries are made in the MGTESR and Engineering Log. If a component that is replaced is a selected equipment, make sure you follow procedures outlined in Naval Ships' Technical Manual, chapter 234, "Marine Gas Turbine Equipment Log Books and Service Records," section 8.

When preparing turn-in components for shipment, plug or cap all openings. Do not take the components apart to look inside. You may cause more damage to the component. The repair activity must decide of cause of failure. Other activities use information on failed components to design improvements.

LM2500 ENGINE CHANGEOUT

At some point in your career, you may have the opportunity to supervise an engine changeout. In this section we will discuss this topic from a supervisory standpoint. For more information on

procedures for engine changeout and post changeout adjustments, you should consult the following technical manuals: The Propulsion Gas Turbine Module LM2500, volume 2, part 3; the Gas Turbine Generator Set, volume 2; and the Team Leader Guide for DD-963 Class Ships, as applicable.

PREPARATION

Planning a full-scale evolution such as a GTE changeout takes effort, coordination, and drive. Careful planning is an essential ingredient to your effective supervision of a GTE changeout. You can reduce delays and confusion by anticipation of the need of escorts and clearances for IMA, civilians, and other personnel involved.

An organizational meeting of all personnel, including those involved with ancillary tasks (crane operators, hook tenders, riggers, and so forth), is necessary to plan the evolution. At the meeting you should inform each individual of his or her responsibility to the overall team effort and how his or her job affects the effort and completion schedule. You should distribute monitoring guides and inventory lists to the parties concerned with an explanation of how and when to use them. During the meeting, you should clarify the time frame established for task completion. Having given personnel clear directions, you can expect them to perform the procedures on schedule. They should not be surprised when you arrive for a checkpoint verification. The most important topic to emphasize is safety. It is your responsibility as team leader to ensure that all safety precautions are strictly followed.

COORDINATION

You can reduce or eliminate the wasting of time by proper coordination of several tasks throughout the changeout. Simple things such as the proper placement of the special support equipment (SSE) containers can eliminate extra walking and moving of components. The SSE containers should be placed within the reach of the crane to avoid unnecessary movement of equipment into a lift area. Crane service must be controlled and used exclusively for the changeout. The engine containers should be brought to the site as soon as possible so they can be opened and ready for installation when scheduled.

Team members must coordinate amongst themselves for certain functions, such as the removing and installation of components and the constant passing of fixtures down and into the module. The importance of communication between team members during the changeout process cannot be overemphasized. One way you can enhance communications is by the team's use of portable radio equipment.

POST CHANGEOUT REQUIREMENTS

With the completion of an engine changeout, you must return the support equipment and the replaced engine. The paperwork involved in the changeout is lengthy, but necessary for proper documentation. Careful preparation of SSE containers and engine containers will ensure they will reach their destination with no damage.

Returning Containers

Returning of the containers with the replaced gas generator and power turbine requires that the major components plus the $T_{5_{,4}}$ and $P_{,5_{,4}}$ harnesses and the speed sensors of that engine are packed within the containers. The completed logbook is also returned with the container. After everything is secured within the containers and the desiccant bags have been dried out/changed, the cover is bolted down and pressurized with nitrogen for shipment. The ship's supply system is responsible for shipping the engine containers to Naval Air Rework Facility (NARF), North Island, California, for refurbishing and testing.

When the SSE containers have been completely inventoried, restacked, and secured, the supply system is responsible for returning the containers to their place of origin. The 56X3 office of Naval Sea Systems Command is notified of the condition of the containers by the team leader via the chain of command.

Reports

Reports from the team leader requires the completion of the record logbook for each component and the proper closeout of that log before stowage in the engine containers. All entries should be complete up to the time of changeout, inventoried to see that they are correct, and signed off by the engineering officer. The SSE containers that were inventoried on arrival are to be inventoried again at completion for reissue to the next user. The engineering officer and main propulsion assistant are required by squadron directives to notify the proper people of any irregularities at the completion of the changeout. If lessons were learned because of the changeout, notify the people concerned with this valuable knowledge.

LESSONS LEARNED

The following section describes some lessons learned during engine changeout.

Pierside Changeouts

Problem areas and past discrepancies during a pierside changeout have been numerous since the first changeout was completed on the old SPRUANCE class ships. Problems, such as location of the equipment and containers at pierside can delay the job. This has happened when equipment or containers are placed out of reach of the crane.

Some changeouts have been hampered by crane service that was not totally dedicated to the job of engine changeout. Many hours were lost awaiting the crane. Crane services are needed full time throughout the changeout. All concerned personnel should realize that to complete the changeout on time, the crane and operator's services are required the full 36 hours. Lifting of the engine is not all that is required of the crane. Every component of the rail system plus all the lift fixtures require crane services. The crane will be in constant use, especially when the personnel basket is used. Personnel are required to check rollers up and down the guide tracks for freedom of movement.

Inclement weather has at times caused difficulties. This is especially true in an unprotected harbor where the water roughness or ground swells have influenced the movement of the ship at the pier. Therefore, to facilitate the changeout, the ship must be pierside and should be inboard of any other ship(s) present. At times, floating cranes have been used. However, the evolution was still hampered by the elements.

Tenderside Changeouts

Tenderside changeouts have problems of a different nature. The tender is a stationary platform. The ship must be moved and positioned around it to help the crane service. The SSE containers, when stored on the tender and within reach of the crane, were on the 03 or 04 level. This made travel to and from them difficult.

Horizontal Rail System

The horizontal rail systems have also had problems. Some of these problems are attributed to their not being inspected before use.

- To ensure safe and proper handling of the engine and/or components by the crane operator, have the ship ballasted to remove any listing.
- Dry trunnion bearings on rail stanchions are difficult to turn. This is especially true if the adjustment ring holes have been elongated. Therefore, a grease lubricant (MLG-G-10924 or equivalent) should be used to lubricate the adjustment ring.
- The horizontal rail flanges, when not properly lined up, will make the gas generator separation hazardous by shifting the gas generator position and possibly damaging the C-sump air seals. On mating up gas generator to power turbine, the number 6 bearing cage can be damaged when the front frame lift fixture roller crosses the forward flange in the rail. This makes the gas generator shift weight.
- The adjustable rollers on the lift fixtures are susceptible to corrosion, thereby jamming the roller in one position. If not properly lubricated before use, the adjustable rollers on the lift fixtures are capable of freezing up. This makes it impossible to center the engine.
- When not properly serviced and filled with cylinder oil, the hydraulic support mechanism for the compressor front frame will not permit the jack to be extended far enough to support the front frame for removal of the support pins.
- Ensure all feeder rail sections are installed and aligned before checking the travel of the system with a hand-held roller.
- If a bearing failure necessitates engine changeout, a complete flushing of the lube oil system is required.

Tag and Bagging Practices

Tag and bagging practices on engine change-outs have not been followed to the letter. This costs time during reassembly. Proper identification is a valuable asset when the new engine is reassembled in place. Lost and broken bolts, in some cases, do not exist as onboard spares. Therefore, exercise care in disassembling and handling to facilitate reassembly. Once bags have been filled and identified, place them in a secure place until they are required for the reassembly.

Replacement Engines

Replacement engines, when received, may not be complete with all the fittings and adapters necessary for connection. In some cases, a replaced engine was in the container and heading for the supply depot before this discovery was made. This caused additional time to be wasted reopening the container and resealing it after the parts or items were removed.

Silencers

Mark the location of the silencer hold-down brackets before removal. Proper marking makes it much easier to reinstall the brackets and silencers.

GTG ENGINE CHANGEOUT

GTG engine changeout procedures are described in detail in the technical manuals, Model J 04 Gas Turbine Generator Set, volume 2, and the Model 139 Gas Turbine Generator Set, volume 2. These procedures provide detailed engine and interference removal instructions.

You must use the same type of planning and engineering practices in GTG engine changeout as you use in LM2500 GTE changeout. The same strict application of safety precautions and following of technical manual procedures apply to GTG engine changeout.

COOPERATION

Ship's readiness is the common purpose in the changeout evolution. All personnel involved should share a common interest in achieving that purpose. A willingness by everyone to submerge his or her personal interest in favor of getting the job done is a prerequisite to cooperation. You may have to adjust working hours and watch-standing duties to meet change-out schedule requirements. Personnel may be assigned to duties they do not want to perform. Emphasize everyone's importance and contribution to the evolution. Engine changeout is an opportunity to display your professional abilities as a leader and technician.

CHAPTER 3

Auxiliary Systems Maintenance

Gas turbine propulsion plants are dependent on reliable auxiliary systems. The proper maintenance and operation of auxiliary systems will enhance the performance of main propulsion machinery. The naval engineering Gas Turbine System Technician (Mechanical) must have a thorough knowledge of main propulsion auxiliary machinery and systems. In this chapter we will describe some of the maintenance, operating problems, and repair of pneumatic systems, low-pressure air compressors (LPAC), hydraulic systems, pumps, valves, heat exchangers, and purifiers.

Before any maintenance or repair work is started, they should consult the manufacturer's technical manuals and maintenance requirement cards (MRCs). These materials contain information concerning specifications, clearances, procedural steps, and troubleshooting techniques of engine-room auxiliary machinery.

Proper maintenance or repair work consists of problem diagnosis, disassembly, measurements, corrections of problems, and reassembly. Use of proper tools, knowledge of the construction of equipment, proper work site management, and cleanliness are keys to successful maintenance and repair work.

Good housekeeping is an integral part of preventive maintenance. Nothing adds more to the impression of a well-maintained plant than cleanliness. Teamwork is required on the part of all hands to maintain a clean plant. Maintenance personnel must realize that the repair job is NOT complete until the old and surplus material has been removed. Assigning specific equipment to individuals and making them responsible for keeping it clean is one effective technique. An individual will take pride in his work and will expect to be reprimanded if he is neglectful. It is difficult for operators to remain concerned in cleaning when improperly designed or maintained equipment continually allows oil or water to leak. If a piece of equipment is designed to leak a fluid, ensure the leakoff remains within specifications.

The technician must ensure that the necessary equipment, tools, and supplies are provided for cleaning. Cabinets for tools, supplies, and lubricants improve the appearance of the plant and facilitate the work.

Work site cleanliness is just as important as space cleanliness. Dirt and foreign matter are just as harmful to machinery as improper lubrication.

Early replacement and/or failure results from inadequate attention to detail during maintenance procedures. Improper materials, wrong clearances, misalignments, or inattention to torque specifications are but a few of the commonly overlooked maintenance requirements. Memory should not be relied upon to determine when an inspection should be made, bearings lubricated, or equipment rotated. Sooner or later something will be neglected, and failure will result, posing a safety problem for personnel and equipment.

COMPRESSED AIR SYSTEMS

Qualifications for lower rates require that you know not only the purpose and principles involved, but also the operation and performance of routine maintenance on auxiliary systems and units that use compressed air. The technicians have already used compressed air for such jobs as starting GTEs, blowing out and cleaning various units, and operating numerous pneumatic tools. If they have worked with any of the three types of compressed air systems (low, medium, and high pressure), you may have found that the principal source of trouble was the compressor. Even though the design and capacity of compressors vary, the maintenance procedures are essentially the same for all of them.

CARE AND MAINTENANCE OF AIR COMPRESSORS

To keep the ship's air compressors operating efficiently always and to prevent as many troubles as possible, you need to know how to care for air intakes and filters; how to maintain and replace air valves; how to take care of air cylinders, pistons, and wrist pins; how to adjust bearings and couplings; and how to properly maintain the lubrication, cooling, control, and air systems.

Air Intakes and Intake Filters

The satisfactory operation of any compressor is based on a supply of clean, cool, dry air. To aid in keeping the air supply clean, filters are fitted to compressor intakes. Unless the filters are inspected and cleaned regularly, they will become clogged and cause a loss of compressor capacity.

Filter elements should be removed from the air intake and cleaned following PMS or technical manual instructions. The filter body should be drained. Fuel oil or other combustible solvents should NEVER be used for cleaning air filters because of the explosive fumes that may collect in the compressor or air receiver.

Air Valves

Air suction and discharge valves are vital parts of a compressor and should receive careful attention. When these valves leak, the compressor capacity is reduced and results in unbalanced stage pressures.

Several symptoms signify when an air valve is not functioning properly. A deviation from normal intercooler pressure, abnormally high intercooler temperatures, and an unusually hot valve cover is a sign of valve trouble.

Broken valve poppets and reeds are major problem areas associated with leaking valves. The source of valve trouble can usually be traced to dirty intake air or excessively high air temperature, resulting from faulty cooling. Periodic inspections and cleaning of valves and valve passages will minimize and perhaps prevent the occurrence of air valve troubles. The frequency for cleaning valves is determined from PMS requirements and the manufacturer's technical manual.

When disassembling a valve, you should note how the various parts are arranged so that the proper relationship will be kept when the valve is reassembled. To clean valve parts, soak each part in a suitable solvent, such as PD-680 dry-cleaning fluid and then brush or scrape lightly. After drying and reassembling the valve parts, test the valve action to ensure the valve opens and closes freely.

Since it is often difficult to distinguish between suction and discharge valves, you should use extreme care when replacing valves. Make sure that suction valves open TOWARD the center of the cylinder, and discharge valves open AWAY FROM the center of the cylinder. If installed improperly, serious damage or loss of compressor capacity will result.

Cylinders and Pistons

When you find that it is necessary to inspect the cylinders or pistons of an air compressor, you should refer to the manufacturer's instruction manual and the appropriate Planned Maintenance System (PMS) MRC for the proper methods and tools required for disassembly and inspection. The following is general information that you can use when checking cylinders or liners, fitting new piston rings, and checking piston end clearance for a vertical compressor.

When inspecting the cylinder or liner, you must take accurate measurements to determine the exact diameter. If the cylinder or liner is worn beyond the manufacturer's recommended limits, it should be replaced. On compressors not equipped with liners, such as air-cooled or large pneumatic service compressors,' one reboring is allowed.

When piston rings are being replaced, they should first be fitted to the cylinder to check for proper end clearance. If necessary, file the ends until the manufacturer's recommended clearance is obtained. Then fit the rings to the piston grooves, making sure that the side clearance of each ring will allow it to fall into the groove by its own weight. Check the thickness of each ring to ensure that the groove is deep enough for the ring thickness. In replacing the rings, ensure they are staggered so that the ring splits are not in line.

After the piston has been replaced in the cylinder, you must check the piston end clearance. The piston end clearance must always be measured and adjusted after replacing the pistons, or after any adjustment or replacement of the main, crank pin, wrist pin, or cross head bearing has been made. You can do this by inserting a lead wire through a valve port or indicator connection and jacking the compressor over so that when the piston has moved to the top of its stroke, the lead will be flattened to the exact amount of clearance at the end of the stroke. Ensure the lead wire is long enough to take a reading at a point near the center of the piston.

In differential piston compressors in which compression takes place in two stages during the same stroke, you must measure the clearance for both stages. In double-acting compressors, or in those compressors in which compression in any stage takes place on the reverse stroke, you must take a second reading of the clearance at the bottom of the stroke of that cylinder.

After taking these readings, you can adjust the piston end clearances. Proper clearances for a specific compressor are usually found in the manufacturer's technical manual or on the blueprint.

For detailed procedures on maintenance overhaul and inspection of air compressors, refer to the manufacturer's technical manual.

ROTARY AIR COMPRESSOR

A nonreciprocating type of air compressor is referred to as a rotary compressor. The rotary air compressor used on board some gas turbine ships is used to supply ship's service low-pressure (LP) air. It is a helical screw-type compressor mounted on a subbase with the following components:

- Drive motor
- Water injection system
- Separator holding tank
- Dehydrator
- Air receivers
- Control system
- Safety devices

These components work together to provide clean, dry, oil-free, LP air to the ship's service air system (SSAS). In this section we will discuss only the compressor.

Compressor Operation

The compressor is driven by an electric motor through a flexible coupling. Air is drawn into the compressor intake pipe through a stainless-steel filter-silencer. The air passes through the unloader valve and into the inlet port of the compressor when the valve is in its open position. Fresh water is injected into the airstream as it passes through the inlet port of the compressor casing. The air then passes axially through the compressor during the compression cycle and is discharged through the outlet port of the compressor casing.

Compressed air from the compressor passes through a short discharge line and check valve, and then into the separator/holding tank where the entrained injection water is removed from the air. The compressed air then leaves the separator/holding tank and passes through a dehydrator where any remaining moisture is removed from the airstream. From the de hydrator, the air passes through a check valve and a back-pressure valve before entering the receiver. Moisture-free air from the receiver is available to the ship's air system on demand.

Compression Cycle

The compression cycle of the compressor starts as the rotors unmesh at the inlet port. As rotation continues, air is drawn into the cavity between the male rotor lobes and the grooves of the female rotor. The air is trapped in these grooves, or pockets, and follows the rotative direction of each rotor. As soon as the inlet port is closed, the compression cycle begins as the air is directed to the opposite, or discharge, end of the compressor. The rotors mesh, which reduces the normal free volume and increases the pressure. This reduction in the volume continues, with a resulting increase in pressure, until the closing pocket reaches the discharge port. Leakage loss of the compressed air is held to a minimum by a combination of safe clearances between the meshing rotors, casing, and end walls, and by fresh water injected into the compressor to both cool the compressed air and seal the necessary running clearances. Since there is no contact between the compressor internal parts, no internal oil lubrication is required. This results in the com pressor discharging oil-free compressed air.

Compressor Bearings

Each rotor shaft rides in its own set of ball and roller bearings. A single caged roller bearing is used at the outlet (or motor) end of the com pressor casing for each rotor shaft. Two thrust ball bearings are used at the inlet end of the casing to support each rotor shaft. These thrust bearings prevent longitudinal movement of the rotors. Splash lubrication is used to oil the rotor shaft bearings and the timing gears. An oil sump is located at each end of the compressor casing. Oil is picked up from these sumps by lubricating discs, or "flingers," located on each end of both rotor shafts. Oil thrown from these flingers is distributed to the timing gear teeth and to all bearing locations. Gravity flow of the oil returns it to the sump.

COMPRESSOR CONTROL DEVICES

Because of the variety of control, regulating, and unloading devices used with compressors, detailed instructions on their adjustment and maintenance must be obtained from manufacturers' technical manuals.

Control Valves

When a control valve fails to work properly, disassembly and a thorough cleaning is usually necessary. Some control valves are fitted with filters filled with sponge material or woolen yarn to prevent dust and grit from being carried into the valve chamber.

NOTE: DO NOT use cotton as a filter element because it will pack down and stop the airflow.

Relief Valves

Since relief valves are essential for the safe operation of a compressed air system, they must always be kept in satisfactory working condition. Relief valves should be set and tested following PMS requirements.

LUBRICATING AND COOLING SYSTEMS

The maintenance procedures for lubricating and cooling systems in air compressors are like the procedures used for lubricating and cooling systems in internal combustion engines.

Lubricating Systems

The lubricating systems of compressors will give you little trouble if the following steps are taken:

1. Keep the reservoir oil at the prescribed level to maintain the proper oil temperature.
2. Change the crankcase oil periodically, flush the crankcase, and clean the oil filter.
3. Maintain proper LO pressure by keeping the oil pump in good working condition and by adjusting the bypass relief valve.
4. Keep the oil cooler free from leaks to prevent oil contamination and emulsification.

Cooling Systems

The general requirements for care and maintenance of compressor cooling systems are as follows:

1. Inspect intercoolers and aftercoolers periodically.
2. Remove collections of gummy oils or tarry substances on the sides of cooler tubes by washing the tube nests with a cutting solution. Be sure that the nests are completely dry before reassembly.
3. Repair any leaks in tube nests; otherwise, water will leak into the compressor while it is secured, and air will leak into the water side during operation.

If during operation, a water relief valve on the coolers blows while the cooling water pressure is normal, most likely a tube in the cooler is ruptured. Secure the compressor immediately and plug the tube, if possible.

4. Inspect and clean cylinder water jackets periodically with a cleaning nozzle.
5. When the cooling water system of the com pressor is being refilled, open the water inlet valve slightly to allow the water to rise slowly in the cooler shell and water jackets. To prevent the formation of air pockets, open the vent valves to allow entrapped air to escape.

CARE AND MAINTENANCE OF AIR SYSTEM EQUIPMENT

You must periodically surface inspect the air flasks and separators to determine any external corrosion or damage to the flasks or piping.

Corrosion

Because of a corrosion-resistant coating, corrosion is seldom a source of trouble on the internal surfaces of air flasks; however, corrosion can take place on the external surfaces of air flasks and may be serious enough to weaken the material, especially in high-pressure (HP) flasks. Surface corrosion usually occurs at points that cannot be easily reached for proper cleaning and painting.

Frequently drain air system equipment to prevent excessive accumulations of moisture. This accumulation of moisture causes internal corrosion and fouling of moving parts.

Inspections and Tests

All HP flasks and separators must be inspected, cleaned, tested, and repainted at prescribed intervals by a repair activity. For surface ships, the initial and subsequent intervals should not exceed 12 years. Inspection intervals for separator flasks is every 3 years; however, if there is reason to believe that serious corrosion of either the exterior or the interior of air flasks is occurring, inspect and test the flasks at once.

Periodic examinations are essential to deter mine the condition of air system equipment; these examinations should include not only a complete inspection of the interior and the exterior of flasks and separators, but also ultrasonic inspections and hydrostatic tests. After a thorough cleaning, the flasks that pass the hydrostatic test are given a prescribed internal protective coating, and when necessary, the -exterior is painted.

SAFETY PRECAUTIONS

Competent personnel operating and maintaining any machine keep it performing as efficiently as possible. To achieve peak performance from a compressed air plant, you should take steps to prevent or minimize the occurrence of any condition that might reduce plant capacity or result in serious damage. You should take every possible precaution to prevent potential explosions, especially when operating HP systems. Safety precautions that will aid you in maintaining a plant in satisfactory operating condition are listed below.

1. Minimize the possibility of explosions in an air compressor, discharge line, or receiver by taking steps to prevent or eliminate the following:
   - Dust-laden intake air
   - Presence of oil vapor in the compressor or receiver
   - Leaking or dirty valves
2. Make sure that the compressor intake receives only cool, dry air.
3. Use only prescribed agents for cleaning compressor intake filters, cylinders, or air passages. DO NOT use benzene, kerosene, or other light oils that could vaporize and form a highly explosive mixture when compressed.
4. Secure a compressor immediately if there is an abnormal rise in the temperature of air discharge from any stage.
5. Be sure a relief valve is installed between a compressor and a stop valve, or a check valve is installed between a compressor and the receiver. If there is no relief valve and the compressor is started against a closed valve or a damaged check valve, the air will not be able to escape, and an explosion can result.
6. NEVER leave a compressor station after starting a compressor, especially a new com pressor or one that has been idle for an extended time, until you are positive that the control, unloading, and governing devices are working properly.
7. Do not disconnect any part of a compressor if the system is under pressure. To avoid serious accidents, you should take the following precautions before working on, or removing, any part of a compressor:
   - Leave all pressure gauges open.
   - Ensure the compressor is completely tagged out following ship's directives and PMS requirements.

- Be sure the compressor is completely blown down.
- Ensure all valves between the com pressor and the receiver are closed.

8. Operate a compressor at the recommended speeds and maintain the proper cooling water circulation to prevent damage from excessive temperatures.

9. Drain the circulating water system of a compressor if it will remain idle for an extended period, or if it will be exposed to freezing temperatures.

Dehydrators

Compressed air is used for the operation of automatic controls, clutches, MRG oil systems, fuel oil systems, waste heat, boiler control, and other systems. To prevent failure of these systems, moisture from the compressor must be kept at a minimum; blowing down the compressor separators prevents most of this, but some moisture is carried over.

To aid in the removal of the moisture, two types of dehydrators are generally used: type I refrigerant dehydrators and type II dehydrators that use a desiccant of either silica gel or activated alumina, and that contain electric heating coils to reactivate the desiccant when it becomes saturated with moisture. Type II dehydrators are normally installed in pairs so that one can always be in service while the other is being reactivated.

HYDRAULIC SYSTEMS

The overall efficiency of hydraulic installations used to control or drive auxiliary machinery is dependent upon the size of the installation, the oil pressure, the speed, and the condition of the equipment. The care you give to the hydraulic components of the system is an important factor. Major repair of hydraulic gear, except for piping and fittings, is generally performed at a naval shipyard or by the manufacturer. You are responsible for all routine maintenance. This includes keeping the oil clean, maintaining proper fluid levels, and performing periodic inspections as defined in the PMS requirements.

PIPING AND FITTINGS

Properly installed hydraulic piping and valves are seldom a source of trouble, except for leakage. Some leaks may become serious enough to cause a reduction in the efficiency of the unit. You should make frequent inspections and take necessary steps to eliminate leakage.

If leaks occur at a flanged joint in the line of a hydraulic system, tighten the flange bolts evenly, but not excessively. If the leaks persist, use the standby unit, if available. If not, secure the equipment while the gasket of the leaking flange is being replaced. Make certain that the flange surfaces are cleaned carefully before the gasket is applied. You should NEVER tighten fittings while the system is pressurized.

Relief valves or shuttle valves of a hydraulic system may be sources of trouble. Loss of power may indicate a leaking relief valve. Shuttle valves may stick and fail to cycle. This condition is indicated when oil escapes from the HP side of the line into the expansion tank or when the pressure control fails. When a shuttle valve fails to operate, the stop valves should be closed, and the defective valve repaired.

FLUID SYSTEM

An inspection of an oil sample drawn from a hydraulic system may reveal the presence of metal particles, water, sludge, acidity, or other contaminants. If so, you must drain, flush, and refill the system following current procedures. The presence of foreign particles in the hydraulic system indicates a possible component malfunction, which you should correct before flushing the system. Dispose of contaminated hydraulic fluid according to prevailing instructions.

HYDRAULIC PUMPS

An electric motor rotates the hydraulic pump. Oil under pressure is delivered from the pump to the hydraulic system. Whether the pumps of hydraulic systems are axial or radial pistons, maintenance procedures and operating principles are relatively the same. In general, maintenance information on other types of pumps also applies to hydraulic pumps.

Packing Material

On modern hydraulic pumps, shaft packing materials are of five general classifications: synthetic rubber, fluorinated compounds, silicones, fabric-rubber combinations, and leather. The hydraulic fluid to be sealed determines the type of packing material to be used. Packings for use in hydraulic systems containing petroleum-based fluid cannot be used in systems using phosphate ester fluids and vice versa. Water-glycol fire-resistant fluids and water-petroleum oil-emulsion fluids are generally compatible with any packings designed for petroleum oil.

The success or failure of any packing material depends on more than compatibility of the fluid and the packing material. Other considerations are pressures, shock loads, clearances, surface finishes, temperatures, frequency and the duration of work cycles. Ensure packings are installed in the sequence and the directions given in the instruction manual. You should tighten the packing glands to keep leakage at acceptable levels. However, overtightening increases friction and shortens packing life.

Alignment

Poor alignment between the driving and driven components of a hydraulic system is less likely if the wedges, shims, jacking screws, or adjusting setscrews are properly set and secured when the connected units are installed. However, if a casualty occurs, misalignment may cause severe stress and strain on the coupling and connected parts. Eliminate misalignment as soon as possible by replacing any defective parts and readjusting the installed aligning devices. If this is not done, pins, bushings, and bearings will have to be replaced frequently.

Couplings

Since the pump or motor shaft has no end play, flexible couplings are generally used in hydraulic systems. Such couplings permit satisfactory operation with a slight misalignment, without requiring frequent renewal of parts.

MAINTENANCE

Regular operation, proper lubrication, proper maintenance of all the units, and cleanliness of the fluid are principal requirements for keeping a hydraulic system in satisfactory operating condition. Regular operation of hydraulic equipment prevents corrosion, sludge accumulation, and freezing of adjacent parts. The need for proper lubrication and cleanliness cannot be too strongly emphasized.

You will find detailed instructions on the maintenance of a specific unit from the PMS and the appropriate instruction manual. However, the general information that follows should also be helpful to you.

In attempting to locate the source of any problem in an electrohydraulic system, remember that all problems will be in one of three categories— hydraulic, electric, or mechanical. Isolating a problem into one of these categories is a primary step in locating the source of trouble.

Hydraulic Casualties

These casualties are generally the result of low oil levels, external or internal leakage, clogged lines or fittings, or improperly adjusted valves and other working parts. Do NOT disassemble a unit unless you are certain that the trouble exists within that unit. Unnecessary disassembly can lead to additional trouble because dirt can enter the open system.

Leaks are a frequent cause of trouble in hydraulic equipment. They are generally caused by excessively worn parts, abnormal and continuous vibration, excessively high operating pressures, or faulty or careless assembly. External leaks usually have little effect on the operation of equipment, other than a steady draining of the oil supply; although, even a small leak wastes oil and creates a safety hazard. The resulting unsightly appearance of a machine is indicative of poor maintenance.

External leaks may result from any of the following causes:

- Improperly tightened threaded fittings
- Cross-threaded fittings
- Improperly fitted or damaged gaskets
- Distorted or scored sealing rings, oil seals, or packing rings
- Scored surfaces of working parts

- Improperly flared tube ends
- Flanged joints not sealing squarely

Internal leaks, however, generally result in the unsatisfactory operation of equipment. Large internal leaks are indicated by a loss of pressure and the failure of equipment. Large internal leaks can usually be located by installing a pressure gauge in various parts of the equipment. The location of small leaks generally requires disassembly and visual inspection of the parts. Internal leaks may result from worn or scored valves and bushings or from improperly fitted or damaged gaskets and O-rings.

The symptoms of trouble in a hydraulic system are frequently in the form of unusual noises. Some noises are characteristic of normal operation and can be disregarded, while others are evidence of serious trouble. Even though the exact sound indicating trouble can be learned only through practical experience, the following descriptive terms will give a general idea of the noises that are trouble warnings.

POPPING and SPUTTERING noises indicate that air is entering the pump intake line. Air entering the system at this point may be the result of too small an intake pipe, an air leak in the suction line, a low oil level in the supply tank, cold or heavy oil, or the use of improper oil.

If air becomes trapped in a hydraulic system, HAMMERING will occur in the equipment or in the transmission lines. If hammering occurs, check for improper venting. In some cases, a POUND ING or RATTLING noise occurs as a result of a partial vacuum produced in the active fluid during high-speed operation or when a heavy load is applied. This noise may be unavoidable under the conditions stated and can be overlooked if it stops when the speed or load is reduced. If the noise continues at low speeds or light loads, the system should be vented of air. Air in a hydraulic system can also cause an uneven motion of the hydraulic pistons.

The cause of a GRINDING noise is most likely to be dry bearings, foreign matter in the oil, worn or scored parts, or the overtightness of an adjustment.

HYDRAULIC CHATTER is a term sometimes used to identify noises caused by a vibrating spring-actuated valve, long pipes improperly secured, air in the lines, or the binding of part of the equipment.

If the packing around a moving part is too tight, SQUEALS or

SQUEAKS may occur. This type of noise might also indicate that a high-frequency vibration is being caused by a relief valve.

Electrical Casualties

Although the Electrical engineers are responsible for checking electrical equipment, the gas turbine engineers can help by making a few simple tests when electrical problems occur. Such an oversight as not having a switch in the ON position may be the reason for equipment failing to operate. If the circuit is closed and the equipment still fails to operate, check for blown fuses and tripped circuit breakers. These troubles generally result from an overload on the equipment. If a circuit breaker continues to open, the problem may be damaged equipment, excessive binding in the electric motor, obstruction in the hydraulic transmission lines, or faulty operation of the circuit breaker. Another source of electrical problems may be in the circuit; check for open or shorted leads, faulty switches, and loose connections.

Mechanical Casualties

An electro-hydraulically driven auxiliary may become inoperative because of a mechanical failure. If so, check for improper adjustment or misalignment of parts, shearing of pins or keys, and breakage of gearing, shafting, or linkage. Elimination of troubles resulting from any of these causes should be accomplished following the manufacturer's instructions for that specific equipment.

CENTRIFUGAL AND ROTARY PUMPS

This section contains information on the operation, inspection, and repair of centrifugal and rotary pumps. The gas turbine engineers will be responsible for the operation and maintenance of various pumps in the engine room and other assigned spaces.

CENTRIFUGAL PUMPS

Centrifugal pumps are widely used aboard ship for pumping nonviscous liquids. Centrifugal pumps are not positive displacement pumps. When a centrifugal pump is operating at a constant speed, the amount of water discharged (capacity) varies with the discharge pressure. This relationship is inherent in the pump design. The relationships among capacity, total head pressure, and power are usually expressed by a characteristic curve. Characteristic curves are found in manufacturers' technical manuals. They may also be found on the outline assembly drawings of the pumps.

Capacity and discharge pressure can be varied by a change in the speed; however, centrifugal pumps should be operated at or near their rated capacity and discharge pressure, when possible. Impeller vane angles and the sizes of the pump waterways can be designed for maximum efficiency at only one combination of speed and discharge pressure; under other conditions of operation, the impeller vane angles and the sizes of the waterways are too large or too small for efficient operation. Therefore, a centrifugal pump cannot operate properly for a long time at excess capacity and low discharge pressure. Also, it cannot operate properly at reduced capacity and high discharge pressure.

Note that centrifugal pumps are NOT self-priming. The casing must be flooded before a pump of this type is operated. For this reason, most centrifugal pumps are located below the level from which suction is to be taken. Priming can also be done using another pump to supply liquid to the pump suction. Some centrifugal pumps have special priming pumps, air ejectors, or other devices for priming.

Because of the danger of overheating, centrifugal pumps can operate at zero flow capacity for only a short period of time. The length of time it may run varies with the design characteristics. For example, a fire pump may operate for as long as 15 to 30 minutes before overheating, but a feed-water pump would flash and seize in a few seconds if operated at zero capacity.

Most centrifugal pumps have recirculation lines from the discharge side of the pump back to the source of suction supply. An orifice allows the recirculation of the minimum amount of fluid required to prevent overheating of the pump.

When operating a centrifugal pump, always have a slight leak-off through the packing in the stuffing boxes. This will keep the packing lubricated and cooled. Stuffing boxes are used to prevent the entrance of air into the pump or the liquid from leaking out. The purpose served depends on whether the pump is operating with a positive suction head or is taking suction from a vacuum. If a pump is operating with a positive suction head, the pressure inside the pump is enough to force a small amount of liquid through the packing when the gland is properly adjusted. On multistage centrifugal pumps, in some cases, you will have to reduce the pressure on one or both stuffing boxes. This is done by use of a bleed-offline tapped into the stuffing box between the throat bushing and the packing.

A pump taking suction at or below atmospheric pressure must have sealing water furnished to the packing glands. This ensures the exclusion of air. Allow some of this water to leak off through the packing. Most centrifugal pumps use the pumped liquids as the lubricating, cooling, and sealing medium; however, some pumps use an in dependent external sealing liquid.

When operating a centrifugal pump, open the vents to release entrained air. If the pump needs frequent venting, leave the vents cracked. This permits a desirable continuous leakage of air and water. Pipe the discharge from the vents to the proper drain systems or to the bilges.

Operating Problems

Most centrifugal pump operating problems are caused by improper operation and maintenance. Operational problems and actual failures of centrifugal pumps are usually caused by (1) improper lubrication, (2) worn bearings, (3) worn packing, (4) worn wearing rings, (5) bent shafts, or (6) misalignment.

Maintenance and Repair

The following discussion of maintenance and repair applies to most centrifugal pumps aboard ship. However, some different designs of centrifugal pumps are in use; for specific information on a certain pump, refer to the manufacturer's technical manual furnished with the unit.

INSPECTIONS OF OPERATING PUMPS. — For routine maintenance, you should make frequent inspections of each operating pump. At least once an hour, check that all temperature and pressure gauges are indicating properly. Check for proper leakage from the stuffing boxes.

LUBRICATION. — It is extremely important that the bearings of a centrifugal pump be properly lubricated. Most motor-driven pumps with ball bearings are fitted for grease lubrication. Be sure that you understand the type of lubrication system used on each pump and that each pump is properly lubricated during operation.

STUFFING BOX PACKING. — Although most centrifugal pumps on gas turbine ships have mechanical seals, you should be familiar with stuffing box packing.

The packing in centrifugal pump stuffing boxes is renewed following the PMS. When replacing packing, be sure to use packing of the specified material and the correct size. Stagger the joints in the packing rings so that they fall at different points around the shaft. Pack the stuffing box loosely and set up lightly on the gland, allowing a liberal leakage. With the pump in operation, tighten the glands and gradually compress the packing. It is important to do this gradually and evenly to avoid excessive friction. Uneven tightening could cause overheating and possible scoring of the shaft or the shaft sleeve. Usually you must put in more packing rings after the first ones have been compressed.

On some centrifugal pumps, a lantern ring is inserted between the rings of the packing. When repacking stuffing boxes on such pumps, be sure to replace the packing beyond the lantern ring. The packing should not block off the liquid seal line connection to the lantern ring after the gland has been tightened.

In the packing arrangement, the lantern ring lines up with the liquid seal connection when the gland is tightened.

SHAFT SLEEVES. — On most centrifugal pumps, the shaft is protected at the stuffing box by sleeves. The sleeves are either screwed or keyed to the shaft. Examine the sleeves whenever the pump is opened for inspection or repair. The sleeves must properly fit the shaft to keep water from leaking between the shaft and the sleeves.

The outer surface of the sleeve must remain smooth and free from scores to prevent excessive wear of the packing. Even a slightly worn or scored sleeve should have a finishing cut to smooth the surface. A badly worn sleeve should be replaced.

WATER FLINGERS. — Water flingers are fitted on shafts outboard of the stuffing box glands. They prevent water from following along the shaft and entering the bearing housing. The water flingers must tightly fit the shaft.

WEARING RINGS. — Most centrifugal pumps have both impeller wearing rings and casing wearing rings. The smaller ring fits over the hub of the impeller and turns with it; the larger ring is attached to the casing and is prevented from turning by the semicircular flange or shoulder. A specified clearance must be kept between the two wearing rings. This prevents excessive leakage from the HP side to the LP side of the impeller. Some pumps have wearing rings only on the casing; in this design, a specified clearance is kept between the impeller and the casing wearing ring.

Check wearing ring clearances often. Maintain them within the specified tolerances. The allowable wear in these rings varies with the type of pump and its use. To replace wearing rings, follow the manufacturer's instructions carefully. Improper fitting of the wearing rings or incorrect assembly of the pump can result in serious damage.

BEARINGS. — Worn bearings on centrifugal pumps are a common cause of pump failure. Worn bearings cause excessive wear of the wearing rings and may cause pump misalignment.

Ball bearings are easily damaged by dirt, foreign matter, and corrosive materials. These materials cause the bearing to wear and become noisy. When ball bearings become worn, replace them. The use of vibration analysis can often detect worn bearings before other symptoms occur.

Check sleeve or shell bearings on centrifugal pumps as necessary. Later in this chapter, we describe methods for you to use when checking bearings. When the maximum allowable wear has occurred, replace this type of bearing. For complete detailed instructions on checking and replacing bearings in centrifugal pumps, you should refer to the manufacturer's technical manual.

BUSHINGS. — Whenever a pump is inspected or being repaired, check the clearances of all bushings on the shaft and renew the bushings when necessary. Bearing wear will very likely cause the bushings to wear.

ROTARY PUMPS

Rotary pumps, unlike centrifugal pumps, are positive-displacement pumps. The THEORETI CAL DISPLACEMENT of a rotary pump is the volume of liquid displaced by the rotating elements on each revolution of the shaft. The CAPACITY of a rotary pump is defined as the quantity of liquid (gpm) delivered under specified conditions. Thus, the capacity is equal to the displacement times the speed (rpm) minus the losses. Some causes of losses are slippage, incomplete filling of pumping cavities, and the amount of dissolved gases present in the liquid.

The rotating elements in a rotary pump may have gears, lobes, vanes, screws, cam-and-plunger arrangements, and other devices for trapping the liquid on the suction side and forcing it through the discharge outlet. Rotary pumps with three high-pitch screws are widely used on naval ships. They are used for pumping high-viscosity liquids such as fuel oil and lubricating oil; they function well if the speed of the pump is adjusted to the viscosity of the liquid being pumped. When high-viscosity liquids are pumped, the pump must be operated at a reduced speed, allowing time for the pump cavity to fill.

Operating Problems

Some of the rotary pump operating problems you may encounter in your engineering plant are as follows:

- The pump fails to deliver liquid or fails to deliver the liquid at the rated capacity.
- The pump loses suction.
- The pump requires excessive power to deliver the rated capacity.

Some common causes of faulty operation in rotary pumps are discussed in the following paragraphs.

INSUFFICIENT PRIMING. — Rotary pumps are generally self-priming; however, if a pump is operating with a suction lift exceeding the lift for which it was designed, it may become air-bound or vapor-bound and may not have the self-priming capability.

CLOGGED SUCTION OR DISCHARGE LINES. — Check all valves in the suction and discharge lines to ensure they are open and operating properly. Check the suction strainer (if equipped) to make sure it is not clogged.

AIR LEAKAGE. — Air leakage into the suction side of the pump or the suction piping or manifold will cause improper operation of the pump.

Check the pump stuffing box and the packing on all valve stems in the suction line and suction manifold. Make sure that no air is leaking into the suction side of the system. Ensure that the suction pipe is submerged in the liquid supply.

VAPOR LOCK. — If a suction lift or the temperature of the pumped liquid is too high, partial vaporization may occur. This can cause vapor lock in the suction piping. Vapor lock is most likely to occur in long suction lines with loops and bends. This can also happen if the pump is handling oil that has been recently transferred or heated. Vapor lock will cause noise, vibration, and pressure pulsations in the pump. To remedy vapor lock, line up another tank, using another manifold if possible, and shift the suction. When the pump operates properly, shift suction back to the original tank. Reducing the speed of a rotary pump may help prevent the development of vapor lock.

ENTRAINED GAS. — Air and/or gas entrained in the liquid being pumped will affect the pump capacity. This is true even at zero suction lift, and as pressure in the suction line decreases, the effects of entrained gas become more pronounced. Entrained gas will cause the same noisy operation and pounding in the pump that is caused by vapor lock. Reducing the speed of the pump or heating the oil being pumped may solve the problem.

Air and other gas DISSOLVED in the pumped liquid does not affect the capacity of the pump at zero suction lift. As the pressure in the suction line decreases, the dissolved gas is freed from the liquid and becomes entrained.

EXCESSIVE VISCOSITY. — If the liquid being pumped is too heavy or too viscous for the design of the pump, more power is needed to operate the unit. To correct this problem, reduce either the viscosity of the pumped liquid or the speed of the pump.

IMPROPER DIRECTION OF ROTA TION. — Occasionally, a motor-driven pump will fail to develop discharge pressure after major repairs have been made to the motor. If this happens, ensure that the pump is rotating in the proper direction.

MECHANICAL DEFECTS. — Several mechanical defects may cause serious operating problems in rotary pumps. Some of these problems are misalignment, improper packing, binding of the rotors, a bent shaft, and an improperly adjusted relief valve.

SHAFT ALIGNMENT. — When you install or assemble pumps driven by electric motors, ensure that the unit is aligned properly. Misalignment causes serious operating troubles later. It is necessary to have the rotating shafts of the driver and driven units in proper alignment.

You should check the shaft alignment of a pump frequently, when the pump is opened for repair or maintenance, or if a noticeable vibration occurs. If the shafts are out of line or inclined at an angle to each other, the unit must be realigned. Whenever practicable, check the alignment with all piping in place and with the adjacent tanks and piping tilled.

Some driving units are connected to the pump by a FLEXIBLE COUPLING. Remember that flexible couplings are intended to correct only slight shaft misalignment. Misalignment should never exceed the amount specified by the pump manufacturer. If the misalignment is excessive, the coupling parts are subjected to severe punishment, necessitating frequent renewal of pins, bushings, and bearings.

When the driving unit is connected to the pump by a FLANGE COUPLING, the shafting may require frequent realignment. Misalignment can be indicated by abnormal temperatures, ab normal noises, and worn bearings or bushings.

Wedges, or shims, are sometimes placed under the bases of both the driven and driving units for ease in alignment when the machinery is installed. Jacking screws may also be used to level the units. When the pump or driving unit must be shifted sidewise to align the couplings, side brackets are welded in convenient spots on the foundation, and large setscrews are used to shift the units sidewise or endwise. When the wedges or other packings have been adjusted so that the outside diameters and faces of the coupling flanges run true as they are manually revolved, the chocks are fastened, the units are securely bolted to the foundation, and the coupling flanges are bolted together.

Coupling ALIGNMENTS MUST BE CHECKED from time to time, and misalignments must be promptly corrected. There are three methods employed for checking alignments:

1. Use of a 6-inch scale
2. Use of a thickness gauge
3. Use of a dial indicator

Some types of installations require special methods of handling.

When using a 6-inch scale to check alignments, check the distance between the faces of the coupling flanges at 90-degree intervals. Find the distances between the faces at point a, point b (on the opposite side), point c, and point d (opposite point c). This action will indicate whether the coupling faces are parallel to each other. If they are not parallel to each other, adjust the driving unit or the pump with shims until the couplings check true. While measuring the distances, you must keep the outside diameters of the coupling flanges in line. To do this, place the scale across the two flanges. If the flanges do not line up, raise or lower one of the units with shims. Then, if necessary, shift them sidewise, using the jacks welded on the foundation. The scale should be used at intervals of 90 degrees.

The procedure for using a thickness gauge to check alignments is similar to that for a scale. When the outside diameters of the coupling flanges are not the same, use a scale on the sur face of the larger flange, and then use a thickness gauge between the surface of the smaller flange and the edge of the scale. When the space is narrow, check the distance between the coupling flanges with a thickness gauge. Wider spaces are checked with a piece of square key-stock and a thickness gauge. Revolve the couplings one at a time, and check at 90-degree intervals. If the faces are not true, the shaft has been sprung. Many times, the shafts must be removed and sent to the ship's machine shop for reworking.

When using a dial indicator to check alignment, clamp the indicator to one coupling flange, and then revolve the coupling with the point of the dial indicator on the shaft of the opposite coupling flange. If no variation is shown on the indicator, the coupling is running true. When the coupling with an indicator clamped to it is revolved while the opposite coupling remains still, the degree to which the coupling centers are out of line will be shown. To adjust the centers, loosen the bolts at the unit bases and recheck the alignment. When the alignment is trued, secure the dowel at the unit bases, and then insert and fasten the coupling bolts. Use dial indicators, if possible, when you align a coupling.

PIPING SYSTEMS

Reasonable care must be given to the various piping assemblies as well as to the units connected to the piping systems. Unless the piping system is in good condition, the connected units of machinery cannot operate efficiently and safely. You should be familiar with all the recommended maintenance procedures and observe the safety precautions when working on piping systems. This section presents general information on the maintenance and repair of piping systems.

CARE OF PIPING SYSTEMS

The most important factor in maintaining piping systems in satisfactory condition is keeping joints, valves, and fittings tight. To ensure this condition, you need to make frequent tests and inspections.

Piping should be tested at the frequency and test pressure specified following the PMS and the applicable equipment technical manual. Test pressure must be maintained for a period of time to disclose any leaks or other defects in the system.

Instruction manuals should be available and followed for the inspection and maintenance of piping systems and associated equipment; however, if the manufacturer's instruction manual is not available, you should refer to the Naval Ships' Technical Manual for details of piping maintenance.

Maintenance and Inspections

Maintaining the operational reliability of ships requires that all piping systems be in good operating condition; therefore, early detection and correction of piping defects are of the utmost importance. Fresh water, lube oil, fuel oil, aviation fuel, and pneumatic systems are critical items, and any unnecessary loss of them must be avoided. Early correction of leaks, such as the repair of faulty seats and disks, will reduce the amount of work, time, and material required for repairs. The following items are of extreme importance for the proper operation of valves and piping systems.

1. Surface inspect piping systems at regular intervals following the PMS requirements to detect and eliminate leaks and ensure satisfactory protection from external corrosion.

2. As stated above, refer to the Naval Ships' Technical Manual and the manufacturer's technical manuals for specific information on a particular piping system or component.

3. If specific instructions are not available, all piping in an operating status should be tested quarterly under maximum operating pressure. In addition, a periodic hydrostatic test of 135 per cent design pressure should be applied to the piping. The period between tests should not exceed a maximum of 5 years and should be conducted prior to, or during, the early stages of a scheduled ship overhaul.

4. On ships in the reserve fleet, thoroughly drain all piping not in use and not pressurized for test purposes.

5. Drain holes or orifices are provided in some systems to permit continuous drainage. Check them periodically to guard against their becoming plugged with dirt or other foreign matter.

6. Before pressurizing any portion of a piping system for operation or test purposes, operate all valves except those that would pressurize the system from another source.

7. Ensure that all valves and equipment in the system, or connected to the system being tested, are in the required position or condition.

8. Sudden stoppage or changes in the flow, velocity, or direction of liquids in piping systems will generate high pressure (water ram), which can cause equipment damage. When the pump discharge valve is open to a closed piping system, the pump should not be started. The air present will be compressed and could result in damage to the equipment.

9. Sudden temperature changes in a piping system can cause uneven contraction and expansion, which can develop stresses that will cause material damage or failure. Rapid and excessive temperature changes are the primary causes of gasket failure.

10. You should NEVER use piping to provide footholds or handholds, or to support your weight.

11. All piping should be properly supported through its entire length.

Marine Growth

Rapid fouling of the firemain has been experienced on many ships, especially those ships operating in tropical waters. To minimize fouling of the firemain and to prevent valves from being stuck open or closed, the following procedures are recommended:

1. Quarterly, flush the firemain under full pressure. A high-velocity flow must be used to remove marine growth. The firemain system may be aligned to direct the flow of water from more than one pump in one end of the ship, through a section of the system, while discharging through an adequate number of weather deck fireplugs. This procedure may be changed to reverse the flow through the piping. Flushing should be accomplished in areas where the seawater is clean.

2. NAVSEA has approved a procedure for acid cleaning of firemain piping to remove scale and marine growth. This type of cleaning can be accomplished by a naval shipyard or by an approved contractor. Acid cleaning is satisfactory and is economical because it can be done without dismantling the piping.

GASKETS

It is possible to achieve a tight seal between surfaces of a flanged joint by the perfect mating of machined or ground surfaces; however, this method is costly, impractical, and generally unsatisfactory. To eliminate the necessity for producing and maintaining perfect joint-contact surfaces, relatively inexpensive and replaceable gaskets are used as the sealing element. The proper seal is obtained by the gasket material filling, or flowing, into the grooves or irregularities on the joint-contact surfaces.

For any flange, the type of gasket used will depend on several considerations: gasket characteristics, operating conditions, temperatures, pressures, and mechanical features (bolting, shape of flange) of the flanged assembly. The selection of gaskets for flanged joints should comply with current Navy standards. The appropriate chapter of Naval Ships' Technical Manual contains information pertinent to the use of gasket materials.

Much of the trouble experienced with leaky piping joints is due to poor alignment or improper allowance for expansion. Either of these faults will cause excessive strain on joints. When the joints are not in alignment, you should realign the piping so that the flanges or unions meet properly without being forced. In aligning piping, you must check the pipe supports adjacent to the joint to be connected to determine that the hangers properly support the line. You can correct an improper hanger support by loosening the support and adjusting it to carry an equal share of the load. In some instances, you may have to reface the flanges. Align the piping sections so that you can insert the flange bolts freely without forcing either the bolts or the piping.

The most practical way to cut a full-faced gasket is to lay the sheet packing over the flange and mark the cutting limits by light blows with a ball peen hammer. Cut the bolt holes slightly larger than the bolts so that the gasket will not bulge along the bolt circle. Use a gasket cutter to cut gaskets that fit inside the bolt circle.

Before joining a gasketed joint, clean all bearing and sealing surfaces thoroughly. You should inspect the surfaces for damage from erosion or steam cutting. Reface or replace flanges that show damage. You should not use bolts and nuts that show signs of wear, corrosion, or other imperfections. Ensure all nuts and bolts are coated with an approved anti seize compound.

The first time a joint is put under pressure, inspect it carefully. If any sign of leakage is evident, tighten all bolts in small increments. If leakage continues after a new gasket has been used, investigate other possible causes.

THREADED CONNECTIONS

Threaded connections were used in piping systems in the past to a great extent, but experience has revealed that these connections are susceptible to shock damage and will become loose with excessive vibration. Based on this, the use of threaded connections is not allowed in new construction piping systems on ships built according to Navy specifications.

UNIONS

Unions are designed to seal against leakage under operating conditions. They have a ground joint, metal-to-metal surface, or for HP air and oxygen service, an O-ring seal. The threaded union nut is required only to furnish mechanical strength for the joint. There is no reduction in the pipe-wall thickness as there is with a commercial threaded pipe joint.

When installing new lines of silver-brazed piping that are not over 2 inches in diameter, ensure enough union fittings and union fitting valves are installed to allow repairs or alterations. Vibration may cause union joints to become loose; check them for leakage at regular intervals.

FLARELESS FITTINGS

Flareless fittings are suitable for use in hydraulic service and air service systems at a maximum operating pressure of 3000 psi and a maximum operating temperature of 250 °F. Flareless fittings are installed to conserve space and to reduce weight, installation time, and system cleaning time. Do not use flareless fittings if you do not have enough space to properly tighten the nuts or if you have to remove the equipment or piping for access to the fittings. An exception to this rule is a gauge board, which is designed so that it may be removed as a unit for repairs or alterations. Do not use flareless fittings where you cannot easily deflect the piping to permit assembly and disassembly.

Before assembly, ensure the tubing end is square, concentric, and free of burrs. For an effective fitting, be sure the cutting edge of the sleeve or ferrule bites into the periphery of the tube; You can do this by presetting the ferrule.

VALVES

Valves, like other equipment, require proper care and maintenance. You should correct any problems with them as soon as possible.

CAUSES AND REMEDIES OF VALVE LEAKAGE

Internal valve leakage is a result of the disk and seat failing to make a tight joint and may be caused by one or more of the following reasons:

1. Foreign substances (scale, dirt, waste, or heavy grease) lodged on the seat in such a way that the disk cannot seat. If the obstructing

material cannot be blown through the valves, the valves will have to be opened and cleaned out.

2. Scoring of the seat or disk will occur if you attempt to close the valve on scale, dirt, or corrosion. If the damage is slight, the valve may be made tight by grinding the disk together with the seat; but if the damage is extensive, a cut will have to be made on the disk, and the valve seat ring may have to be renewed.

3. The disk may not seat properly because of a bent spindle guide or a bent valve stem.

4. The valve body or disk may be too weak for the purpose for which it is used, causing distortion of the valve seat or disk under pressure.

5. In valves fitted with seat rings, leakage may occur as the result of leakage around the threads of the seat rings. To correct this defect, remove the seat ring, clean the threads, and remake the joint. You may have to recut the threads in the valve and renew the seat ring to secure tightness.

6. Leakage may be caused by a loose valve disk. When a valve disk comes loose from its stem, the cause is either failure of the securing device or corrosion. The first cause is seldom found in well-constructed valves, and the recurrence of the failure can be prevented by minor adjustments or greater care in the valve reassembly.

Corrosion of valve stems usually occurs to valves installed in saltwater lines. You should inspect the stems showing signs of corrosion periodically so that you can replace them before a failure occurs. Always make the replacements with Monel stems. To prevent failure caused by corrosion, use split pins in valve disks in water lines made of nickel-copper alloy instead of iron, steel, or brass.

When you disassemble a valve for repairs, ensure that the valve will be in proper condition when it is reassembled. During disassembly, take every precaution to prevent damage to the gasket, O-ring sealing area, seating surfaces, and the guiding surfaces. When the valve is disassembled, you should thoroughly clean and inspect all of the parts for excessive wear. Inspect the seating surfaces to determine if lapping, grinding, or machining is required to restore the surfaces to the correct fit. Check the stem carefully for straightness, wear of the packing area, and damage to the threaded section.

If the seating surface is badly corroded or is deeply scored, machining will be necessary. You must use the proper size cutter in the reseating machine and take light cuts until the damaged areas are removed. If the seating surface is made from a metal that is too hard for a reseating machine to cut, the work will have to be done in a lathe. If excessive wear or severe pitting has taken place, the machining required to remove the damage may be extensive enough to warrant installing a new disk.

After the machining is completed, the seating surfaces on metal-to-metal seated valves should be lapped to ensure the smoothest possible finish. The lap must be the exact size and shape as the valve disk so that the valve seating surface will be true.

When reassembling the valve, use new gaskets and packing. Ensure all parts move freely as the assembly progresses. Do not tighten the packing nut more than necessary to prevent excessive leakage.

When new valve parts are required, the parts must be the same as those originally used.

PRESSURE REDUCING VALVES

Several types of pressure reducing valves are installed on Navy ships. Some of the maintenance procedures for these valves are discussed in the following paragraphs.

Pneumatic Reducing Valves

Pneumatic pressure-controlled reducing valves are pressure-balanced valves that require a supply of air or gas under pressure for the motive force. The most probable causes of erratic operation of these valves are incorrect pressure in the loading dome or an accumulation of dirt or other foreign matter on the surface of the moving parts. You can correct loading pressure by either increasing or decreasing the pressure of the control gas or air to maintain the proper outlet pressure.

If the cause of improper operation is the presence of dirt or other foreign matter, the only remedy is to disassemble the valve and clean all the parts. You may disassemble the valve in place or remove it from the piping and disassemble. When the valve is disassembled, clean all parts with an approved solvent and a bristle brush or soft cloth. NEVER USE AN ABRASIVE MATERIAL TO CLEAN VALVE PARTS. If the usual cleaning methods will not remove hardened deposits of oil or other foreign matter, clean the part by scraping it with a sharp tool; however, use extreme caution to prevent damage to the surface finishes. Give particular attention to cleaning all guide surfaces to ensure that all moving parts will move freely without binding.

Another possible source of trouble is leakage around the seating surfaces of the disk and seat ring and the joint between the seat ring and the body. If leakage occurs at these points, the valve will not operate properly. You must make a careful inspection of these surfaces, and if leakage is present, you may recondition the seat ring and disk by lapping or grinding. If the joint between the seat ring and the body is leaking, you must install a new seat ring.

You must inspect all parts for excessive wear, paying attention to the valve spring and the diaphragm spring. If either part is broken or weakened, you must install a new spring.

When the valve is reassembled and installed, test it by opening the outlet valve and cracking the inlet valve to thoroughly warm up the valve. Pressurize the dome with air or gas at approximately 10 psig more than the desired outlet pressure.

Spring-Loaded Reducing Valves

Another type of reducing valve that you will encounter is the spring-loaded type that is installed in flushing and cooling water systems. It is a single-seated, direct-acting, and diaphragm type.

Failure of this type of valve can usually be traced to one or more of the following causes:

1. A ruptured diaphragm
2. Leakage through the disk seat or seat ring threads
3. Ports plugged with dirt or other foreign matter
4. Grooves worn in the bore of the sleeve
5. Leaking cup leather

If the diaphragm ruptures, there will be no control of the valve. The diaphragm can be renewed without removing the valve from the piping system.

To repair the valve, remove all tension from the adjusting spring, and then remove the diaphragm nuts from their bolts. Next, lift the spring chamber from the valve body, providing access to the diaphragm, which can now be removed. Install a new one and reassemble the valve. The diaphragm should always be renewed when deterioration is indicated.

Any time disassembly of the valve becomes necessary, all parts of the valve should be cleaned and inspected for excessive wear. You can clean the parts with an approved solvent and a soft brush.

Give attention to cleaning the guide surfaces between the seat ring and ring guides and to the guide surfaces of the sleeve.

The setting surface of the seat ring should need little repair, but if it is scored or otherwise damaged, lap it, using the same process as described for other valves. If the damage to the seating area is excessive or the bore is badly worn, install a new seat ring.

If there are signs of deterioration of the disk seat, renew it. If a new disk seat is not available, turning the seat over will provide a new seating surface; however, this should be considered as a temporary repair, and a new disk seat should be installed as soon as it is available.

If the cup leather shows signs of leaking or deterioration, renew it. Inspect the bore of the sleeve for excessive wear or corrosion. If there is excessive damage to the sleeve, renew it. If the sleeve is only slightly damaged, correct the damage by machining the surface in a lathe. The bore should be concentric, with a smooth finish and not enlarged so much that leakage will occur when the cup is installed.

RELIEF VALVES

Relief valves are installed on piping and units of machinery where an excessive pressure may build up and damage equipment or endanger personnel. Relief valves are adjusted to lift at the proper pressure by an increase or decrease in the compression of the spring.

Failure of the valve to function properly is usually caused by an incorrect setting of the spring, leakage between the disk and seat, leakage around the threads of the seat ring, misalignment of the disk stem, or an accumulation of dirt or other foreign matter around the guiding parts.

Relief valves may usually be disassembled in place, or they may be removed from the piping when repairs are necessary. The first step in disassembling a relief valve is to release all tension on the adjusting spring. This is done by loosening the locknut, and then loosening the adjusting screw. (Some relief valves are fitted with a test lever which must be removed before the spring tension can be released.) Remove the top assembly by unscrewing the head bolt nuts and lifting the head from the body of the valve (depending on the construction of the valve). Then, remove the disk and inspect the seating surfaces. Recondition the seating surfaces by lapping, grinding, or machining in the same manner as you would seat a glove valve.

You should inspect all surfaces used for guide purposes for burrs, galling, excessive wear, or other defects which may interfere with the free movement of the working parts. Replace parts that are worn excessively, bent, or unfit for further service. When you replace parts, always use manufacturer-produced replacement parts.

When a relief valve has been overhauled, you should test it for leaks before installing it in the piping system or on a unit of machinery. It is easier to mount the valve on a test stand (if available) and conduct a hydrostatic test and set the relieving pressure at the desired amount, than to set it after installation.

On some relief valves, an adjusting ring has been provided so that the reseating pressure and the relieving pressure can be adjusted. The position of the ring may be raised or lowered in relation to the disk by the removal of the adjusting ring setscrew and moving of the ring to the desired position. Raising the ring will increase the blowdown period and lowering the ring will decrease the blowdown period.

DIAPHRAGM CONTROL VALVES WITH AIR-OPERATED PILOTS

Diaphragm control valves with air-operated control pilots are being used increasingly on newer ships for various pressure-control applications.

These valves and pilots are available in several basic designs to meet different requirements.

Many of these air-operated control valves are constructed with handwheels for manual operation if an air pressure loss or malfunction occurs in the control system. Depending on the specific system criteria, these valves and control systems are designed to fail in one of three positions upon a loss of air pressure. They will fail in the open position, closed position, or the selected position at the time of the failure.

You should always consult the manufacturer's instruction manual for information on any repair or calibration of air-operated control systems.

HYDRAULIC VALVE MAINTENANCE

Valves are used in hydraulic systems to control the rate of flow, the direction, and the pressure of the fluid. Hydraulic valves are usually named or identified by the function, capacity (size), and pressure rating. In some instances the identity of the valve may reflect a feature of its construction such as a needle valve (characterized by a long tapered valving element) or a servo valve (basically a variation of an electrically operated directional valve, using a small electrical signal to control a relatively large flow of fluid). Maintenance of the hydraulic valves is ensuring that all valve parts are clean and in good condition. Any imperfections of the parts should be corrected as soon as they are noticed. Leakage through the valve will increase quite rapidly due to erosion. Maintenance and repair procedures must follow the PMS and the equipment technical manuals.

You should observe the following precautions when performing maintenance on hydraulic valves:

1. Perform all maintenance in a clean, uncluttered area.
2. Be careful not to reverse the ends of the spool and sleeve after removing them from the valve body. (Each spool is matched to its sleeve by the manufacturer.)
3. Before removing a spool from its sleeve, matchmark the ends with marking pencil, chalk, or tape. NEVER matchmark with a prick punch.

4. While the spool and sleeve are out of the body, keep them wrapped in lint-free cloths to protect the finished surfaces.

5. NEVER replace only a spool or a sleeve. If one piece requires replacement, replace both pieces with a spare matched set.

6. NEVER lap or grind a spool or sleeve.

7. Clean the parts of hydraulic valves with lint-free cloths.

8. NEVER use compressed air to clean out the ports or bore of a hydraulic valve. Particles in the air stream will abrade the seating surfaces.

HEAT EXCHANGERS

Any device or apparatus designed to allow the transfer of heat from one fluid (liquid or gas) to another fluid is a heat exchanger. Waste heat boilers (WHB), bleed air coolers, and lube oil coolers are primary examples of heat exchangers; in common usage, however, waste heat boilers are seldom referred to as heat exchangers.

For heat to transfer from one substance to another, there must be a difference in the temperature of the two substances. Heat flow or heat transfer can occur only from a substance that is at a higher temperature to a substance that is at a lower temperature. When two objects at different temperatures are placed in contact with each other, or near each other, heat will flow from the warmer object to the cooler one until both objects are at the same temperature. Heat transfer occurs at a faster rate when there is a large temperature difference than when there is only a slight temperature difference. As the temperature difference approaches zero, the rate of heat flow also approaches zero.

Some heat exchangers RAISE THE TEMPERATURE of one fluid. Fuel oil heaters, combustion air preheaters, lube oil heaters, and many other heat exchangers used aboard ship serve this function.

Other heat exchangers LOWER THE TEMPERATURE of one fluid. Lube oil coolers, boiler water sample coolers, and masker air coolers are examples of this type of heat exchanger.

Condensers REMOVE LATENT HEAT from a fluid to make it change from a gas to a liquid. Very often, the latent must be removed without removal of any sensible heat—that is, the state of the fluid is changed without lowering the temperature of the liquid. For example, the purpose of the WHB control condenser is to remove the latent heat from steam so that the steam will condense. In this process, however, the temperature of the condensate is not lowered by more than a few degrees. Since any heat removed from the condensate must be replaced in the boiler, lowering the temperature of the condensate is a waste of heat. In addition, the hotter the condensate, the less oxygen it can absorb.

Some heat exchangers ADD LATENT HEAT to a fluid to make it change from a liquid to a gas. The generating part of a boiler is a good example of this type of heat exchanger.

CLASSIFICATION OF HEAT EXCHANGERS

Heat exchangers may be classified according to the path of heat flow, the relative direction of the flow of the fluids, the number of times that either fluid pass each other, and the general construction features, such as the type of surface and the arrangement of component parts. The types of heat exchangers in common use in naval ships are described in the following sections in terms of these basic methods of classification.

Path of Heat Flow

When classified according to the path of heat flow, heat exchangers are divided into two basic types. The INDIRECT or SURFACE type of heat exchanger allows the heat to flow from one fluid to the other through a tube, plate, or other sur face that separates the two fluids, with no mixing of the fluids. In the DIRECT-CONTACT type of heat exchanger, the heat is transferred directly from one fluid to another as the two fluids mix. The deaerating feed tank is a direct-contact heat exchanger; practically all other heat exchangers used aboard ship are of the indirect or surface type.

Direction of Fluid Flow

In surface heat exchangers the fluids may flow parallel to each other, counter to each other, or at right angles to each other (crossflow).

PARALLEL FLOW. — In the parallel flow type both fluids flow in the same direction. If a parallel flow heat exchanger has a lengthy heat transfer surface, the temperatures of the two fluids will be practically equal as the fluids leave the heat exchanger.

COUNTERBLOW. — In the counterflow type the two fluids flow in opposite directions. Counterflow heat exchangers are used in many applications that require large temperature changes in the cooled or heated fluids. Fuel oil heaters, lube oil coolers, and many internal-combustion engine coolers are examples of the counterflow type.

CROSSFLOW. — In the crossflow type, one fluid flows at a right angle to the other. Crossflow is useful for removing latent heat, thereby condensing vapor to liquid. Crossflow is used for most condensers, including main and auxiliary condensers.

Counterflow and crossflow heat exchangers are more commonly used than the parallel flow aboard ship. In many heat exchangers, the types of flow are combined in various ways so that it is difficult to determine whether the flow is parallel, counter, or cross.

Number of Passes

Surface heat exchangers may be classified as SINGLE-PASS units if one fluid passes another only once, or as MULTIPASS units if one fluid passes the other more than once. Multipass flow may be obtained either by the arrangement of the tubes and the fluid inlets and outlets, or using baffles to guide the fluid so that it passes the other fluid more than once before it leaves the heat exchanger.

Type of Surface

Surface heat exchangers are known as PLAIN SURFACE units if the surface is relatively smooth, or as EXTENDED SURFACE units if the surface is fitted with rings, fins, studs, or some other kind of extension. The main advantage of the extended surface unit is that the extensions increase the heat transfer area without requiring any substantial increase in the overall size and weight of the unit.

Type of Construction

Surface heat exchangers are often given names that indicate general features of design and construction. Most surface heat exchangers are of the SHELL-AND-TUBE construction; however, the shell-and-tube arrangement is modified in various ways and it may not be easy to recognize the basic design. Shell-and-tube heat exchangers include such types as the (1) straight tube, (2) U-bend tube, (3) helical or spiral tube, (4) double tube, (5) strut tube, and (6) plate tube heat exchangers.

STRAIGHT TUBE. — In straight-tube heat exchangers, the tubes are usually arranged in a bundle and enclosed in a cylindrical shell. The ends of the tubes may be expanded into a tube sheet at each end of the bundle, or they may be expanded into one tube sheet and packed and ferruled into the other. The ferrules allow the tube to expand and contract slightly with temperature changes.

U-BEND TUBE. —U-bend-tube heat ex changers, sometimes called RETURN BEND heat exchangers, consist of a bundle of U-shaped tubes inside a shell. Since the tubes are U-shaped, there is only one tube sheet. The shape of the tubes pro vides enough allowance for expansion and contraction.

HELICAL OR SPIRAL TUBE — Helical- or spiral-tube heat exchangers have one or more coils of tubing installed inside a shell. The tubes may be attached to headers at each end of the shell. In relatively simple units, such as boiler water sample coolers, the ends of the tubing may pass through the shell and serve as the inlet and the outlet for the fluid that flows through the coil of tubing.

DOUBLE TUBE. — Double-tube heat ex changers have one tube inside another. One fluid flows through the inner tube and the other fluid flows between the outer and the inner tubes. The outer tube is the shell for each inner tube. The shells, or outer tubes, are usually arranged in banks and are connected at one end by a common tube sheet with a partitioned cover that serves to direct the flow. Many double-tube heat exchangers are of U-bend construction to allow for expansion and contraction. The sectional G-fin fuel oil heater, commonly used by the Navy, is an example of a double-tube heat exchanger.

STRUT TUBE AND PLATE TUBE. — Strut-tube and plate-tube

heat exchangers are different in design from the other shell-and-tube heat exchangers. The tubes in the strut-tube and plate-tube heat exchangers consist of pairs of flat, oblong strips that allow one fluid to flow inside the tubes and the other fluid to flow around the outside. Strut-tube and plate-tube heat exchangers are used primarily as water coolers and lube oil (LO) coolers in internal-combustion engines; they can also be used as LO coolers for some auxiliary machinery.

MAINTENANCE OF HEAT EXCHANGERS

Foreign matter lodged on or in the tubes of a heat exchanger interferes with and reduces the rate of heat transfer from one fluid to the other. Heat exchangers requiring the most attention are those where the cooling medium is seawater. Marine growth can form on the tube surfaces and, in extreme cases, completely block the flow.

The seawater side of the tubes should be cleaned as often as necessary. The intervals will depend on the rate that slime, marine growth, scale, mud, oil, grease, and so forth, are deposited on the tube walls. The amount of such deposits depends upon existing conditions. Operation in shallow water, for example, may cause this type of fouling of the tubes.

The resistance of heat exchanger tubes to corrosion depends on a thin, adherent, continuous film of corrosion products on the surface exposed to seawater; therefore, you must be extremely careful when cleaning the tubes not to use abrasive tools capable of marring or scratching the surface of the tube. You should never use wire brushes or rubber plugs having metal parts inside con denser tubes. Any scratch or perforation of the corrosion-resisting film will form a pit that will widen and deepen. Eventually this can result in tube failure (through corrosion pitting), in the same manner as occurs when foreign matter lodges on the tube surface.

For ordinary cleaning, push an air lance through each tube, wash the tube sheets clean, and remove all foreign matter from the water chests. In installations with severe fouling, push a water lance through each tube to remove foreign matter. For extreme fouling, you should run a rotating bristle brush through each tube—or drive soft rubber plugs, available at shipyards, through the tubes by using air or water pressure. After wards, ensure this procedure is followed by water-lancing.

ZINCS

Where zinc anodes are required to protect the heat exchanger materials from electrolysis, good metallic contact must exist between the anodes and the metal of the condenser.

A casual inspection of a badly scaled zinc anode, especially while it is still wet, may lead personnel to believe that the metal is exposed instead of the scale. The anode, even though it appears to be in good condition, should be cleaned with a chipping hammer to learn the true condition of the metal. Whenever zincs are inspected or cleaned, check the condition of the metallic con tact between the anode and its support.

OIL COOLERS

Oil coolers should be operated as required to maintain the oil (inlet) temperature to the bearings at the designed value. With the bearing orifices properly adjusted and the bearings in the proper operating condition, the temperature of the oil on the discharge side of the cooler should satisfactorily meet all normal operating conditions.

When the system has more than one cooler, the coolers should be used alternately and for about the same number of hours.

Maintenance of Lube Oil Coolers

With reasonable care, LO coolers installed on Navy ships will remain in service for several years. When saltwater is used as the cooling medium, failure is usually caused by erosion due to high water velocity or by corrosion due to electrolytic action.

All coolers are built according to NAVSEA specifications. These specifications are designed to give adequate cooling with seawater velocities below those that cause appreciable erosion.

Reports of failure of this type of equipment are rare in comparison with the number of coolers installed in naval ships. Most cooler failures have occurred to units that are supplied with cooling water from a service main, with the supply of seawater to the cooler limited only by a valve or an orifice in the supply line. If the pressure sup plying the cooler is too high, it will cause excessive velocity through the cooler and may result in failure due to erosion. At the same time the oil temperature is usually not appreciably lower than that obtained with proper seawater flow.

Of the two causes of cooler failure, the most likely one will be erosion from the high velocity of seawater. To get satisfactory service from these units, you should ensure the following precautions are taken:

1. Limit the seawater flow to the minimum that is consistent with maintaining the oil temperature within limits specified by NAVSEA or as given in the manufacturer's technical manual.
2. When securing a cooler for an extended period, drain the saltwater side and flush with fresh water, if practicable. All other times keep the cooler flooded and periodically flushed with saltwater.
3. Clean in the manner prescribed by NAVSEA.

The above precautions apply to other heat transfer equipment such as bleed air coolers, air compressor interstage and afterstage coolers, and other coolers that use seawater as a cooling medium.

Cleaning Lube Oil Coolers

If a lubricating system should become contaminated with saltwater, the system must be thoroughly cleaned before it is returned to service. The cooler must be disassembled, and all traces of rust, scale, and other foreign matter removed; otherwise serious damage will result.

With the proper use of LO purifiers, filters, and strainers, normally, only the saltwater sides of the shell and tube coolers need to be cleaned. You should use air-lancing or water-lancing, and if necessary, a round, bristle brush. Under NO circumstances use a WIRE BRUSH for this purpose.

You can clean tube bundles that have been removed by flushing them with hot water; however, do not chemically clean shell and tube coolers without the express approval of NAVSEA.

AIR COOLERS

Air coolers are used for closed-circuit cooling of machinery. In this type of cooler, the air is circulated repeatedly. The advantages of closed-circuit cooling versus open-circuit cooling, where the atmospheric air is passed through the machine, include the following:

1. The machine is cleaner because it is protected from any harmful gases or moisture that may be present in the outside air.
2. Fire risks are low because the oxygen content of the enclosed air is insufficient to sustain combustion.
3. Cooling of the machine is independent of the outside air.

Maintenance of Air Coolers

The air cooler is a double-tube cooler. The double-tube construction enables leaks in the water tubes to be detected before a serious tube failure occurs.

Each double-tube consists of a water-carrying tube surrounded by a close-fitting outer tube. Axial grooves in the inside surface of the outer tube extend the full length of the cooler. The grooves in the tubes all open into TEL-TALE chambers at each end of the cooler. If a leak occurs in one of the main water-carrying tubes, the leakage runs into the groove in the surrounding tube; from there it runs into one of the tell-tale chambers. This arrangement is designed to prevent water leakage into the air ducts of the machine. Leakage can be detected by a discharge from the open ends of the tell-tale drain tubes.

To obtain continuous service from the air coolers, you must operate and maintain the equipment properly. Inspections and preventive maintenance are invaluable in locating and preventing trouble before serious damage can result.

Cleaning of Air Coolers

The air cooler must be cleaned whenever foreign matter interferes with the flow of air across the tubes or whenever water deposits impair the flow of water through the tubes. Accumulations of foreign matter inside or outside the tubes will prevent proper heat transfer. You must clean the cooler at least every 6 months. To clean the air cooler, use the following steps:

1. Close the valves in the water lines to and from the air cooler. Drain the water from the cooler.

2. Disconnect the water, vent, drain, and telltale connections.
3. Clean the water passages using the following procedures:
   - Ordinary cleaning. Push an air lance through each tube, wash the tube sheets, and remove all foreign matter from the water chests.
   - Severe fouling. Push a water lance instead of an air lance through each tube.
   - Extreme fouling (resulting from oil or grounding of a ship). Run a rotating bristle brush through each tube or use soft rubber plugs driven through the tubes by air or water pressure. Complete the process using a water lance.

NOTE: You should NEVER use abrasive tools that could scratch or mar the tube surface. Any local scratch in the thin film of corrosion products on the surface of the tubes could form the nucleus of a pit of corrosion which may widen, deepen, and cause tube failure.

4. Clean the outside of the tubes with com pressed air.
5. Reassemble, using new gaskets.

CENTRIFUGAL PURIFIERS

Centrifugal purifiers are used to purify fuel oil and lubricating oil. A purifier may be used to remove water and sediment from the oil, or to remove sediment only. When water is involved in the purification process, the purifier is usually called a SEPARATOR. When the principal item of contamination is sediment, the purifier is used as a CLARIFIER. Purifiers are generally used as separators for purifying fuel oils. When used to purify lubricating oil, the purifier may be used as either a separator or a clarifier. Whether the purifier is used as a separator or as a clarifier depends on the moisture content of the oil being purified.

Oil that contains no moisture requires that it be clarified only since the oil will be discharged in the purified state after the solids have been deposited in the bowl of the purifier. If the oil contains some moisture, the continued feeding of "wet" oil into the bowl will eventually result in a water-filled bowl. This prevents any further separation of water from the oil. The layer of water in the bowl reduces the depth of the oil layer before the bowl is filled with water. As a result, the incoming oil will pass through the bowl at an increased velocity. The liquid is now subject to centrifugal force for a shorter time, preventing the complete separation of water from the oil. For this reason, the centrifuge should NOT be operated as a clarifier unless the oil contains little or NO water. A small amount of water can be accumulated, together with the solids, and drained when the bowl is stopped for cleaning. If an appreciable amount of water is still in the oil, the purifier should be operated as a separator.

TYPES OF CENTRIFUGAL PURIFIERS

There are two types of purifiers used on naval ships. Both types operate on the same principle; however, the difference is in the design of the rotating units. In one type, the rotating element is a bowl-like container which encases a stack of disks, and the other type of rotating element is a hollow, tubular rotor. These two types of purifiers are known as the disk-type purifier and the tubular-type purifier.

DISK-TYPE PURIFIER

In the sectional view of a disk-type centrifugal purifier, the bowl is mounted on the upper end of the vertical bowl spindle, which is driven by a worm wheel and friction clutch assembly. A radial thrust bearing at the lower end of the bowl spindle carries the weight of the bowl spindle and absorbs any thrust created by the driving action.

Contaminated oil enters the top of the revolving bowl through the regulating tube. The oil passes through the inside of the tubular shaft and out at the bottom into the stack of disks. As the dirty oil flows up through the distribution holes in the disks, the high centrifugal force exerted by the revolving bowl causes the dirt, sludge, and water to move outward and the purified oil to move inward toward the tubular shaft. The oil passes through the disks, rises underneath the top disk, and passes into the tubular shaft. The water forms a seal between the top disk and the bowl top. (The top disk is the dividing line between the water and the oil.) The disks divide the space within the bowl into many separate narrow passages or spaces. The liquid confined within each passage is restricted so that it can flow only along that passage. This arrangement prevents excess agitation of the liquid as it passes through the bowl and creates shallow settling distances between the disks.

Most of the dirt and sludge remains in the bowl and collects in a uniform layer on the inside vertical surface of the bowl shell. Any water, along with some dirt and sludge that is separated from the oil, is discharged through the discharge ring at the top of the bowl. The purified oil flows inward and upward through the disk, discharging from the neck of the top disk.

Tubular-Type Purifier

A cross section of a tubular-type centrifugal purifier is a type of purifier consisting of a hollow rotor or bowl which rotates at high speeds. The rotor has an opening in the bottom to allow the dirty lube oil to enter and has two sets of openings at the top to allow the oil and water (separator), or the oil by itself (clarifier), to discharge. The bowl, or hollow rotor, of the purifier is connected by a coupling unit to a spindle which is suspended from a ball bearing assembly. The bowl is belt-driven by an electric motor mounted on the frame of the purifier.

The lower end of the bowl extends into a flexible mounted guide bushing assembly. The assembly restrains movement of the bottom of the bowl. It does allow enough movement so that the bowl can center itself about its center of rotation. Inside the bowl is a device consisting of three flat plates equally spaced radially. This device is commonly referred, to as the three-wing device, or the three-wing. The three-wing rotates with the bowl and forces the liquid in the bowl to rotate at the same speed as the bowl. The liquid to be centrifuged is fed, under pressure, into the bottom of the bowl through the feed nozzle so that the liquid jets into the bowl in a stream.

When the purifier is used as a LO clarifier, the three-wing has a cone on the bottom, against which the feed jet strikes to bring the liquid smoothly up to bowl speed without making an emulsion.

The separation process is basically the same in the tubular-type purifier as in the disk-type purifier. In both types, the separated oil assumes the innermost position, and the separated water moves outward. Both liquids are discharged separately from the bowls. The solids separated are retained in the bowl.

GENERAL NOTES ON PURIFIER OPERATIONS

You should obtain specific details of operating a given purifier from the appropriate instructions provided with the unit. The information you have been provided is general and applicable to both types of purifiers.

For maximum efficiency, purifiers should be operated at the maximum designed speed and rated capacity. Since reduction gear oils are usually contaminated with water condensation, the purifier bowls should be operated as separators and not as clarifiers.

When a purifier is operated as a separator, PRIMING OF THE BOWL with fresh water is essential before any oil is admitted into the purifier. The water serves to seal the bowl and to create an initial equilibrium of liquid layers. If the bowl is not primed, the oil will be lost through the water discharge port.

Influencing Factors in Purifier Operation

There are several factors that influence purifier operation. The time required for purification and the output of a purifier depend on such factors as the viscosity of the oil, the pressure applied to the oil, the size of the sediment particles, the difference in the specific gravity of the oil and the substances that contaminate the oil, and the tendency of the oil to emulsify.

The viscosity of the oil will determine the length of time required to purify the oil. The more viscous the oil, the longer the time will be to purify it to a given degree of purity. Decreasing the viscosity of the oil by heating is one of the most effective methods of facilitating purification.

Even though certain oils may be satisfactorily purified at operating temperatures, a greater degree of purification will generally result by heating the oil to a higher temperature. To accomplish this, the oil is passed through a heater where the proper temperature is obtained before the oil enters the purifier bowl.

Oils used in naval ships may be heated to specified temperatures without adverse effects, but prolonged heating at higher temperatures is not recommended because of the tendency of such oils to oxidize. Oxidation results in rapid deterioration. In general, oil should be heated sufficiently to produce a viscosity of approximately 90 seconds Saybolt Universal (90 SSU).

Pressure should NEVER be increased above normal to force a high-viscosity oil through the purifier. Instead, viscosity should be decreased by heating the oil. The use of excess pressure to force oil through the purifier will result in less efficient purification. On the other hand, a reduction in the pressure that the oil is forced into the purifier will increase the length of time the oil is under the influence of centrifugal force and will result in improved purification.

The proper size discharge ring (RING DAM) must be used to ensure the oil discharged from a purifier is free of water, dirt, and sludge. The size of the discharge ring used depends on the specific gravity of the oil being purified. All discharge rings have the same outside diameter, but have inside diameters of different sizes. Ring sizes are indicated by even numbers; the smaller the number, the smaller the ring size. The size, in millimeters, of the inside diameter is stamped on each ring. Sizes vary in 2-millimeter steps. Charts provided in manufacturers' technical manuals specify the proper ring size to be used with an oil of a given specific gravity. Generally, the ring size indicated on the chart will produce satisfactory results; however, if the recommended ring fails to produce satisfactory purification, you may have to determine the correct size by trial and error. The most satisfactory purification of the oil is obtained when the ring used is the largest possible size that will prevent the loss of oil with the discharged water.

Maintenance of Purifiers

To properly care for oil purifiers, you should clean them frequently and carefully remove all sediment from the bowl. The frequency of cleaning depends on the amount of foreign matter in the oil. The machine should be shut down for examination and cleaning daily, or more often if necessary. The amount of sediment found in the bowl will give an indication of how long the purifier may be operated between cleanings.

When the purifier is operating on the sump of an operating unit, you should make frequent checks to ensure that the purifier has not lost its seal. A loss of lube oil casualty can occur rapidly if the lube oil is dumped to the bilge or drain tank by an improperly operating purifier.

SUMMARY

In this chapter, you have been presented information that describes the basics of auxiliary systems maintenance. These support systems, such as air compressors, lubricating and cooling systems, hydraulic systems, and their associated piping systems are integral components of the engineering plant. Without the proper maintenance of these auxiliary systems, the mission of the ship cannot be accomplished.

The maintenance and repair procedures described in this chapter are by no means complete or inclusive. Specific clearances, repair procedures, and operating instructions must be researched through the manufacturers' technical manuals and the applicable Naval Ships' Technical Manual for specific clearances, repair procedures, and operating instructions.

INDEX

Printed in the United States
By Bookmasters